180 DAYS® of Reading for Third Grade

Authors

Alyxx Meléndez

Melissa Laughlin

Contributing Authors

Christine Dugan, M.A.Ed.
Jodene Lynn Smith, M.A.

Program Credits

Corinne Burton, M.A.Ed., *President* and *Publisher*
Emily R. Smith, M.A.Ed., *SVP of Content Development*
Véronique Bos, *Vice President of Creative*
Lynette Ordoñez, *Content Manager*
Ashley Oberhaus, M.Ed., *Content Specialist*
David Slayton, *Assistant Editor*
Jill Malcolm, *Graphic Designer*

Image Credits: p.11 Shutterstock/Andrzej Lisowski Travel; p.67 Shutterstock/A.RICARDO; p.68 Shutterstock/Photo Works; p.211 Shutterstock/Krysja; all other images Shutterstock and/or iStock

Standards

Shell Education
A division of Teacher Created Materials
5482 Argosy Avenue
Huntington Beach, CA 92649
www.tcmpub.com/shell-education
ISBN 979-8-7659-1805-0

Printed by: 584728
Printed in: India
PO#: 22679

Table of Contents

Introduction

The Need for Practice

To be successful in today's reading classroom, students must deeply understand both concepts and procedures so that they can discuss and demonstrate their understanding. Demonstrating understanding is a process that must be continually practiced for students to be successful. According to Robert Marzano, "Practice has always been, and always will be, a necessary ingredient to learning procedural knowledge at a level at which students execute it independently" (2010, 83). Practice is especially important to help students apply reading comprehension strategies and word-study skills. *180 Days of Reading* offers teachers and parents a full page of reading comprehension and word recognition practice activities for each day of the school year.

The Science of Reading

For some people, reading comes easily. They barely remember how it happened. For others, learning to read takes more effort.

The goal of reading research is to understand the differences in how people learn to read and find the best ways to help all students learn. The term *Science of Reading* is commonly used to refer to this body of research. It helps people understand how to provide instruction in learning the code of the English language, how to develop fluency, and how to navigate challenging text and make sense of it.

Much of this research has been around for decades. In fact, in the late 1990s, Congress commissioned a review of the reading research. In 2000, the National Reading Panel (NRP) published a report that became the backbone of the Science of Reading. The NRP report highlights five components of effective reading instruction. These include the following:

- **Phonemic Awareness:** understanding and manipulating individual speech sounds
- **Phonics:** matching sounds to letters for use in reading and spelling
- **Fluency:** reading connected text accurately and smoothly
- **Vocabulary:** knowing the meanings of words in speech and in print
- **Reading Comprehension:** understanding what is read

There are two commonly referenced frameworks that build on reading research and provide a visual way for people to understand what is needed to learn to read. In the mid-1980s, a framework called the Simple View of Reading was introduced (Gough and Tunmer 1986). It shows that reading comprehension is possible when students are able to decode (or read) the words and have the language to understand the words.

The Simple View of Reading

Decoding × Language Comprehension = Reading Comprehension

Another framework that builds on the research behind the Science of Reading is Scarborough's Reading Rope (Scarborough 2001). It shows specific skills needed for both language comprehension and word recognition. The "strands" of the rope for language comprehension include having background content knowledge, knowing vocabulary, understanding language structure, having verbal reasoning, and understanding literacy. Word recognition includes phonological awareness, decoding skills, and sight recognition of familiar words (Scarborough 2001). As individual skills are strengthened and practiced, they become increasingly strategic and automatic to promote reading comprehension.

The Science of Reading *(cont.)*

Many parts of our understanding of how people learn to read stand the test of time and have been confirmed by more recent studies. However, new research continues to add to the understanding of reading. Some of this research shows the importance of wide reading (reading about a variety of topics), motivation, and self-regulation. The conversation will never be over, as new research will continue to refine the understanding of how people learn to read. There is always more to learn!

180 Days of Reading has been informed by this reading research. This series provides opportunities for students to practice the skills that years of research indicate contribute to reading growth. There are several features in this book that are supported by the Science of Reading.

Text Selection

- Carefully chosen texts offer experiences in a **wide range of text types**. Each unit includes nonfiction, fiction, and a nontraditional text type or genre (e.g., letters, newspaper articles, advertisements, menus).
- Texts intentionally build upon one another to help students **build background knowledge** from day to day.
- Engaging with texts on the same topic for a thematic unit enables students to become familiar with related **vocabulary**, **language structure**, and **literacy knowledge**. This allows reading to become increasingly strategic and automatic, leading to better **fluency** and **comprehension**.

Activity Design

- Specific **language comprehension** and **word-recognition skills** are reinforced throughout the activities.
- Each text includes a purpose for reading and an opportunity to practice various reading strategies through annotation. This promotes **close reading** of the text.
- Paired fiction and nonfiction texts are used to promote **comparison** and encourage students to **make connections** between texts within a unit.
- Students **write to demonstrate understanding** of the texts. Students provide written responses in a variety of forms, including short answers, open-ended responses, and creating their own versions of nontraditional texts.

This book provides the regular practice of reading skills that students need as they develop into excellent readers.

How to Use This Resource

Unit Structure Overview

This resource is organized into twelve units. Each three-week unit follows a consistent format for ease of use.

Week 1: Nonfiction

Day 1	Students read nonfiction and answer multiple-choice questions.
Day 2	Students read nonfiction and answer multiple-choice questions.
Day 3	Students read nonfiction and answer multiple-choice, short-answer, and open-response questions.
Day 4	Students read a longer nonfictional text, answer multiple-choice questions, and complete graphic organizers.
Day 5	Students reread the text from Day 4 and answer reading-response questions.

Week 2: Fiction

Day 1	Students read fiction and answer multiple-choice questions.
Day 2	Students read fiction and answer multiple-choice questions.
Day 3	Students read fiction and answer multiple-choice, short-answer, and open-response questions.
Day 4	Students read a longer fictional text, answer multiple-choice questions, and complete graphic organizers.
Day 5	Students reread the text from Day 4 and answer reading-response questions.

Week 3: Nontraditional Text

Day 1	Students read nontraditional text and answer multiple-choice and open-response questions.
Day 2	Students complete close-reading activities with paired texts from the unit.
Day 3	Students complete close-reading activities with paired texts from the unit.
Day 4	Students create their own nontraditional texts.
Day 5	Students write their own versions of the nontraditional text from Day 1.

How to Use This Resource *(cont.)*

Unit Structure Overview *(cont.)*

Paired Texts

State standards have brought into focus the importance of preparing students for college and career success by expanding their critical-thinking and analytical skills. It is no longer enough for students to read and comprehend a single text on a topic. Rather, the integration of ideas across texts is crucial for a more comprehensive understanding of themes presented by authors.

Literacy specialist Jennifer Soalt has written that paired texts are "uniquely suited to scaffolding and extending students' comprehension" (2005, 680). She identifies three ways in which paired fiction and nonfiction are particularly effective in increasing comprehension: the building of background knowledge, the development of vocabulary, and the increase in student motivation (Soalt 2005).

Each three-week unit in *180 Days of Reading* is connected by a common theme or topic. Packets of each week's or each unit's practice pages can be prepared for students.

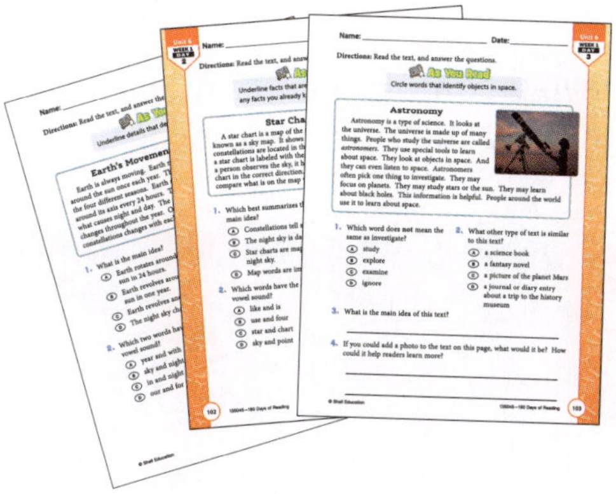

During Week 1, students read nonfictional texts and answer questions.

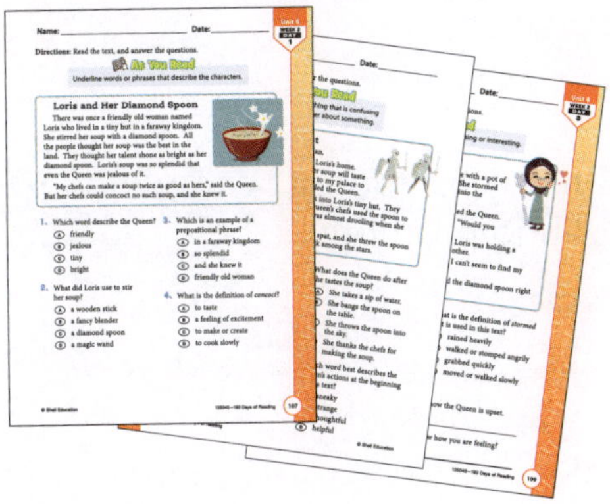

During Week 2, students read fictional texts and answer questions.

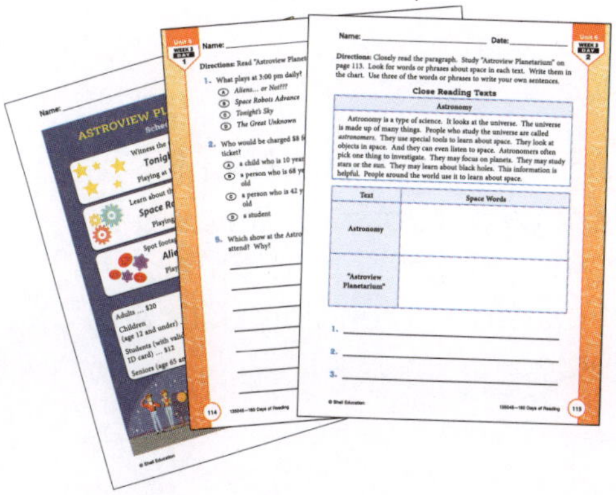

During Week 3, students read nontraditional texts (advertisements, poems, letters, etc.), answer questions, and complete close-reading and writing activities.

How to Use This Resource *(cont.)*

Student Practice Pages

Practice pages reinforce grade-level skills across a variety of reading concepts for each day of the school year. Each day's reading activity is provided as a full practice page, making them easy to prepare and implement as part of a morning routine, at the beginning of each reading lesson, or as homework.

Practice Pages for Weeks 1 and 2

Days 1 and 2 of each week follow a consistent format, with a short text passage and multiple-choice questions.

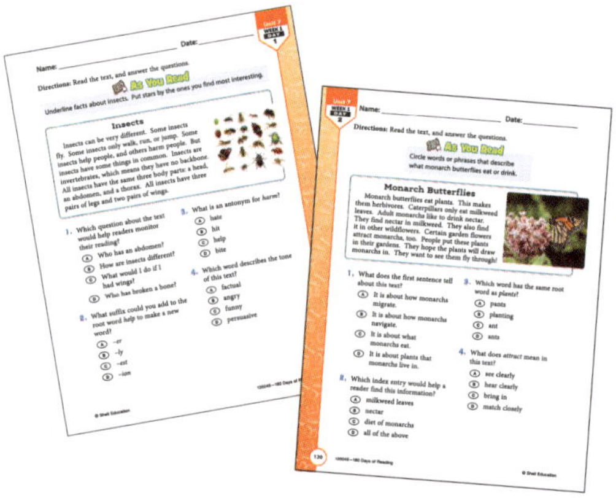

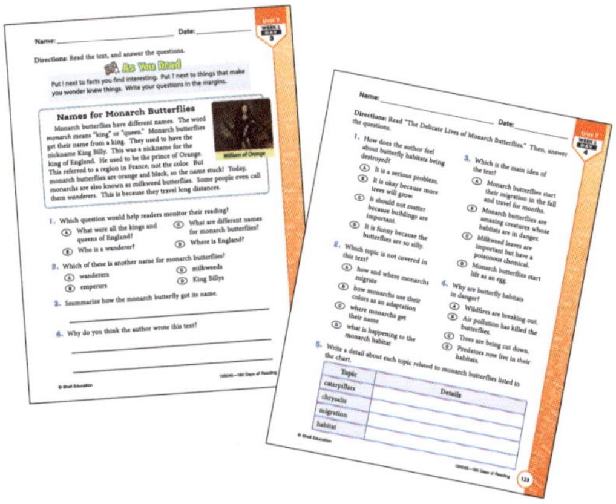

Days 3 and 4 have a combination of multiple-choice, short-answer, and open-response questions.

On day 5, students complete text-based writing prompts.

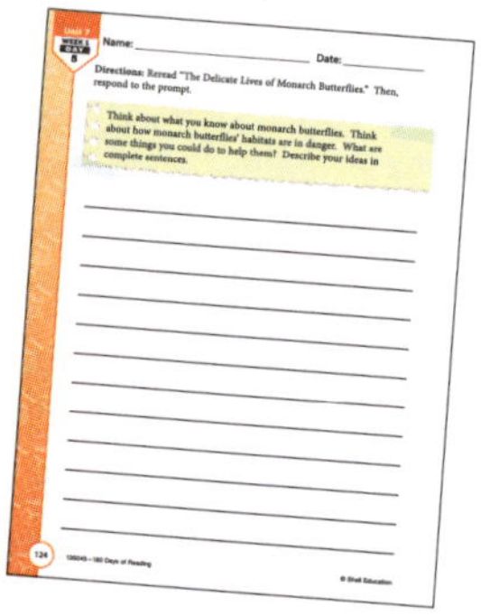

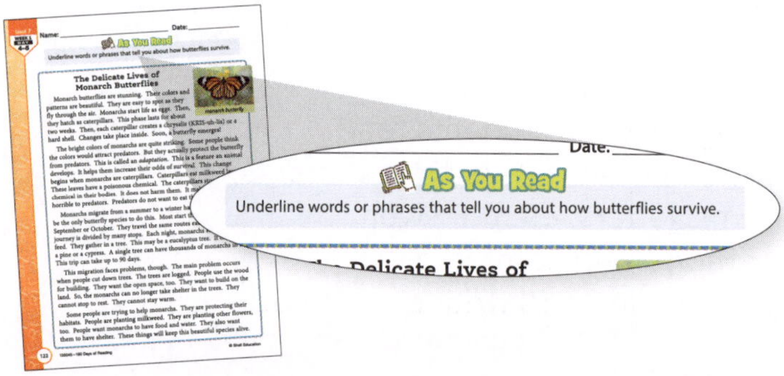

The As You Read activities give students a purpose for reading the texts and provide opportunities to practice various reading skills and strategies.

How to Use This Resource *(cont.)*

Student Practice Pages *(cont.)*

Practice Pages for Week 3

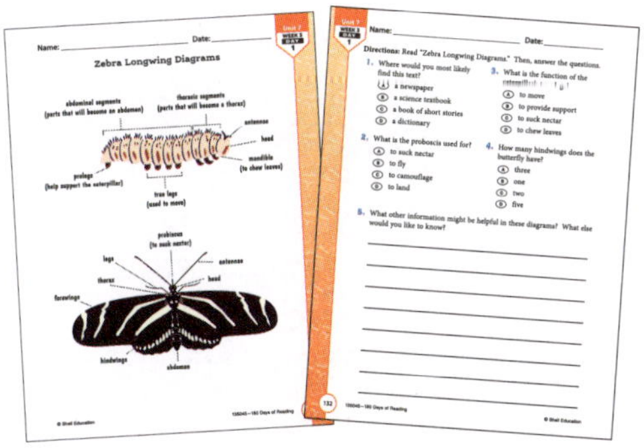

Day 1 of this week follows a consistent format, with a nontraditional text and multiple-choice and open-response questions.

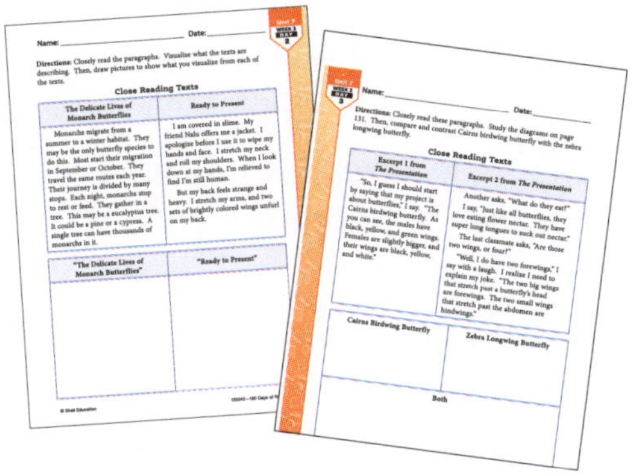

On days 2 and 3, students engage in close-reading activities of paired texts. Students are encouraged to compare and contrast different aspects of the texts they read throughout the unit.

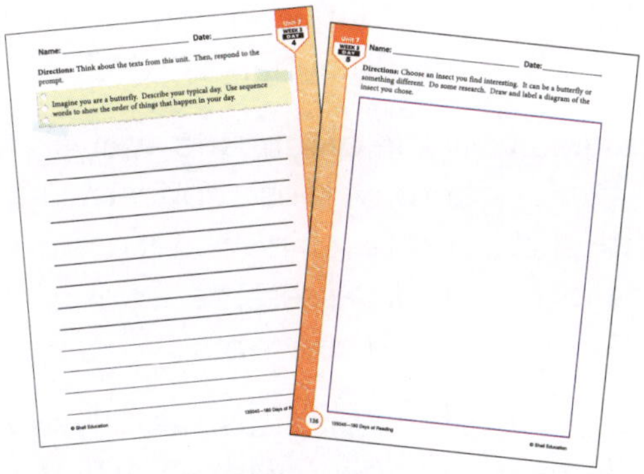

On days 4 and 5, students think about the texts in the unit, respond to a writing prompt, and construct their own versions of diverse texts. Students are encouraged to use information from texts throughout the unit to inspire and support their writing.

Instructional Options

180 Days of Reading is a flexible resource that can be used in various instructional settings for different purposes.

- Use these student pages as daily warm-up activities or as review.
- Work with students in small groups, allowing them to focus on specific skills. This setting also lends itself to partner and group discussions about the texts.
- Student pages in this resource can be completed independently during center times and as activities for early finishers.

How to Use This Resource *(cont.)*

Diagnostic Assessment

The practice pages in this book can be used as diagnostic assessments. These activity pages require students to think critically, respond to text-dependent questions, and utilize reading and writing skills and strategies. (An answer key for the practice pages is provided starting on page 230.)

For each unit, analysis sheets are provided as *Microsoft Word®* files in the digital resources. There is a *Class Analysis Sheet* and an *Individual Analysis Sheet*. Use the file that matches your assessment needs. After each week, record how many answers each student got correct on the unit's analysis sheet. Only record the answers for the multiple-choice questions. The written-response questions and graphic organizers can be evaluated using the writing rubric or other evaluation tools (see below). At the end of each unit, analyze the data on the analysis sheet to determine instructional focuses for your child or class.

The diagnostic analysis tools included in the digital resources allow for quick evaluation and ongoing monitoring of student work. See at a glance which reading genre students may need to focus on further to develop proficiency.

Using the Results to Differentiate Instruction

Once results are gathered and analyzed, use the data to inform the way to differentiate instruction. The data can help determine which concepts are the most difficult for students and that need additional instructional support and continued practice.

The results of the diagnostic analysis may show that an entire class is struggling with a particular genre. If these concepts have been taught in the past, this indicates that further instruction or reteaching is necessary. If these concepts have not been taught yet, this data is a great preassessment and demonstrates that students do not have a working knowledge of the concepts.

The results of the diagnostic analysis may also show that an individual or small group of students is struggling with a particular concept or group of concepts. Consider pulling aside these students while others are working independently to instruct further on the concept(s). You can also use the results to help identify individuals or groups of proficient students who are ready for enrichment or above-grade-level instruction. These students may benefit from independent learning contracts or more challenging activities.

Writing Rubric

A rubric for written responses is provided on page 229. Display the rubric for students to reference as they write. Score students' written responses, and provide them with feedback on their writing.

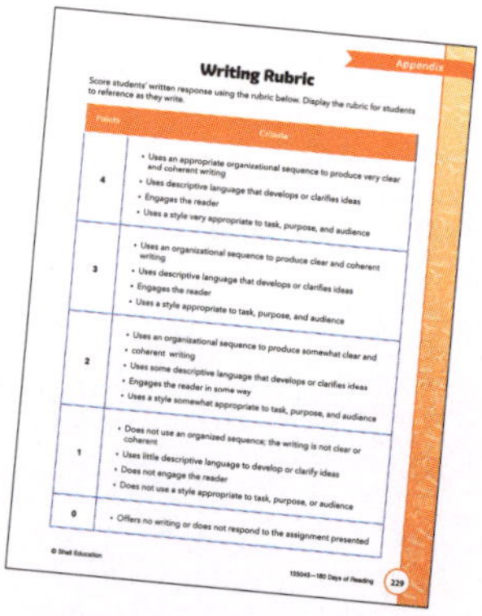

Name: ______________________________ Date: ______________

Directions: Read the text, and answer the questions.

As You Read

Underline important facts about Sir Edmund Hillary.

The Amazing Sir Edmund

Sir Edmund Hillary was an amazing man. He was the first person to reach the top of Mount Everest. He did this in 1953. He was very curious about that part of the world. He returned to the area after his climb. He raised funds for small towns near Everest. This money helped people build bridges and schools. Hospitals were also built. He worked hard to make the world better.

1. Which image would tell a reader more about this text?

- (A) a photograph of a school
- (B) a picture of money used in this part of the world
- (C) a chart showing the number of homes built
- (D) a photograph of a town near Everest

2. What does *raised* mean in this text?

- (A) collected
- (B) built
- (C) high
- (D) lifted

3. What is the definition of *funds* as it is used in this text?

- (A) supplies
- (B) accounts
- (C) treasures
- (D) money

4. What is the author's opinion of Sir Edmund Hillary?

- (A) The author doubts his achievements.
- (B) The author respects him.
- (C) The author does not understand him.
- (D) The author is confused by him.

Name: ______________________________ Date: ______________

Directions: Read the text, and answer the questions.

As You Read

Put a ! next to facts you find interesting. Put a ? next to facts that make you wonder new things.

Mt. Everest

Mount Everest is a tall mountain. It is on the border of Tibet and Nepal. India is nearby. There are many tall summits in the area. The 10 tallest peaks in the world are there. The peaks are quite old. Mount Everest was formed sixty million years ago. It is still growing! It grows about 2 inches (51 millimeters) every year.

1. What topic is the main focus of this text?

- (A) Tibet
- (B) Nepal
- (C) Mt. Everest
- (D) old peaks

2. Which word would most likely be found in the glossary of this text?

- (A) years
- (B) summits
- (C) grows
- (D) still

3. Which word is a synonym for *peaks*?

- (A) trees
- (B) curves
- (C) mountain tops
- (D) plants

4. What type of text would include language similar to what is used in this text?

- (A) a social studies book
- (B) a joke book
- (C) a letter
- (D) a thank-you note

Name: ______________________________ Date: ______________

Directions: Read the text, and answer the questions.

As You Read

Circle the words that identify climbing gear.

Gear for the Climb

Mountain climbers have to wear special gear to protect them. They wear a lot of layers that help them stay warm. This includes gloves, hats, and glasses. They also use special tools. One tool is an ice axe that helps break up the ice. A regulator is a tool that provides oxygen to climbers. They need this at the tops of peaks where the air is low in oxygen. Each climber also needs a radio in case they have to call for help.

mountain climber breathing through a regulator

1. What is the author's purpose?
   - (A) to teach about a mountain climber's gear
   - (B) to make people laugh about tools
   - (C) to compare mountain climbers to rock climbers
   - (D) to share a biography of a famous climber

2. Which of these words has the root word *ice*?
   - (A) icicle
   - (B) nice
   - (C) rice
   - (D) incident

3. What is a regulator?

   ____

4. Which piece of gear do you think is most important? Why?

   ____

   ____

Name: ______________________ Date: ______________

As You Read

Underline information that is new or interesting to you.

Climbing Mt. Everest

A climber heads up Mt. Everest.

Mt. Everest is the tallest mountain in the world. It is over 29,000 feet (8,839 meters) tall. It is in the central Himalayas. Mt. Everest is on the border of Tibet and Nepal.

People are very interested in climbing this amazing peak. The mountain has become a challenge for some. Getting to the top of Mt. Everest is not easy. People have to train a lot. The altitude requires special attention. There is not much oxygen that far up. People's bodies have to adjust. Climbing takes time. Their bodies have to get used to the low oxygen levels.

The Mt. Everest base camps are where climbers begin to climb. These camps are on opposite sides of Mt. Everest. They are also very high. They are more than 16,000 feet (4,877 meters) high. Climbers rest at the base camps. They pack and get their supplies ready before they begin climbing. There are other camps on the way to the peak. It takes a while to reach each camp. Climbers spend time at the camps. This helps them adjust to the elevation.

The highest part of the mountain is called the *summit*. It is covered with deep snow. The snow stays there all year. It is very cold up there! The wind can also blow very hard. This makes the climb pretty risky. Climbers have to be careful. They have special gear. This keeps them warm. It also keeps them from falling.

There are people who work to help climbers. They are called *sherpas*. They carry tents. They also cook food. They work at this job to support their families. Sherpas often get help from yaks. Yaks are strong animals. They help transport goods up the mountain.

Reaching the summit is an amazing feat. Not many humans are able to do such a difficult task. Sadly, not everyone survives the trek up Mt. Everest. More than 200 people have died climbing the mountain. This sad fact reminds people of the danger in climbing.

It is a dream of many to stand on the top of Mt. Everest. It takes bravery and hard work to do it.

Name: ______________________ Date: ______________

Directions: Read "Climbing Mt. Everest." Then, answer the questions.

1. What is the author's purpose for readers?

- (A) to be entertained
- (B) to be persuaded to climb a mountain
- (C) to learn about Mt. Everest and mountain climbing
- (D) to learn about climate change

2. What statement would the author likely agree with?

- (A) Climbing is too dangerous to try.
- (B) Everyone should try to climb Mt. Everest.
- (C) Climbing Mt. Everest is an amazing adventure.
- (D) Traveling that far to climb a mountain is silly.

3. The first paragraph of the text ________.

- (A) introduces the topic
- (B) describes a problem
- (C) compares and contrasts two famous mountains
- (D) does not fit with the rest of the text

4. What is one reason climbers are brave?

- (A) They help sherpas earn a living.
- (B) They do good things for Earth.
- (C) Climbing is a dangerous hobby.
- (D) They do not know what they are doing.

5. Write three facts from the text to support the main idea.

Main Idea	Mt. Everest is an amazing place, and people who climb it are brave and strong.
Detail	
Detail	
Detail	

Name: ______________________ Date: ______________

Directions: Reread "Climbing Mt. Everest." Then, respond to the prompt.

Climbing Mt. Everest is a huge task. It requires special planning and a lot of courage. Would you like to climb Mt. Everest? Why or why not? Use details from the text to support your answer.

Name: ______________________________ Date: ______________

Directions: Read the text, and answer the questions.

As You Read

Underline words and phrases that tell you about Earth's Crust, a character in the story.

Flat Crust

A long, long time ago, Earth's Crust was flat. No hills or mountains rose above the horizon. No caves or valleys plunged beneath the ground. The Crust liked being flat.

"This way, all the animals will live equally," said the Crust. "No beast will be higher or lower than another. And everything will be simple."

But the animals did not like living on the Crust. They were tired of the Crust's flat routine. When the animals told jokes, the Crust did not laugh. When the animals invited the Crust to celebrate a special day, the Crust did not join.

"No day should be more special than any other day," said the Crust.

1. Which statement is true about the Crust?

- (A) It loves to tell jokes.
- (B) It likes everything to be flat and simple.
- (C) It wants to build mountains and valleys.
- (D) It does not like the animals.

2. What is the meaning of *flat* in the sentence, "They were tired of the Crust's flat routine"?

- (A) boring
- (B) smooth
- (C) bumpy
- (D) angry

3. What type of text is this?

- (A) friendly letter
- (B) poetry
- (C) nonfiction
- (D) fiction

4. Which of these words has the same root word as *plunged*?

- (A) planter
- (B) lunge
- (C) plunging
- (D) lodge

Name: ______________________ Date: ______________

Directions: Read the text, and answer the questions.

As You Read

Underline words and phrases that tell you about the Core, a new character in the story.

Fiery Core

Under the Crust, Earth's Core was always in motion. Molten rock bubbled and boiled inside it. The Core liked to move and change nonstop.

"All things will change in the end," said the Core. "Each day is different from the last. It's best to be prepared for any situation."

The Crust disagreed. "If I make sure every day is the same, I won't have to prepare for change." And the Crust tried its best to make sure every day was the same. Thick layers of rock protected the Crust from the Core's fiery magma. But one day, a long, long time ago, the Core got a little too excited. Those thick layers of rock cracked. In an instant, everything changed, and the Crust was never the same again.

1. Which statement would the Core most likely agree with?
   - (A) Change is scary.
   - (B) Change is bad.
   - (C) Change is good.
   - (D) Change will never happen.

2. What happens when the Core gets too excited?
   - (A) Layers of rock crack.
   - (B) Magma bubbles.
   - (C) Core yells at the Crust.
   - (D) The Crust gets excited.

3. Which statement describes the relationship between the Crust and the Core?
   - (A) They are brothers.
   - (B) They are friendly, but disagree.
   - (C) They agree on everything.
   - (D) They are enemies and disagree.

4. Which word is a synonym for the verb *change*?
   - (A) stay
   - (B) middle
   - (C) reverse
   - (D) alter

Name: ______________________________ Date: ______________

Directions: Read the text, and answer the questions.

As You Read

Visualize what is happening in the text.
Underline words or phrases that help you do this.

A Different Earth

Jets of glowing lava erupted from Earth's Crust. Plants caught on fire, and animals fled their homes in panic. The air filled with smoke and screeches. The once-smooth Crust was now covered in bubbling, burning cracks.

"I'll never forgive you, wretched Core. You've destroyed everything," cried the Crust.

"You know I couldn't stop the flow of magma inside me, dear Crust. It could not be contained. Some things have been destroyed, but other things will be created. All of Earth will find balance again. You'll forgive me in time," the Core said calmly.

1. What is most likely happening in the first paragraph?

- (A) A storm is causing damage.
- (B) The Crust and Core are fighting.
- (C) A tidal wave is crashing.
- (D) A volcano is erupting.

2. What do you think *wretched* means in the text?

- (A) happy and excited
- (B) very mean or bad
- (C) friendly
- (D) scared or fearful

3. The first paragraph has a lot of descriptive language. Read it again. Draw what you visualize.

Name: ______________________________ Date: ______________

As You Read

Underline words or phrases that describe how things changed on Earth.

How Earth Changed

Earth's Crust held a grudge against Earth's Core for millions of years. Lava kept flowing out of the Core and onto the Crust. It cooled and formed mountains on land and islands in the sea. The land slowly moved. Animals made their homes on these new landforms, and the animals began to change. Some goats moved to tall mountains and changed their hooves into shapes perfect for cliff climbing. Some fish moved to dark caves. They never saw sunlight after that, so they stopped bothering to have eyes.

"This is just what I was afraid of," the Crust complained. "The animals won't respect each other. One will always be higher or lower than another."

"Higher doesn't mean better," warned the Core. "Higher means closer to the Sky, and lower means closer to you and me. Is it bad to be closer to me?"

"Well, I don't like being close to you. The animals probably feel the same," said the Crust.

"We don't feel the same," said a herd of elephants.

"We quite like our new homes," said an army of frogs.

The Crust couldn't believe what it heard. "But you will face more challenges. Storms, droughts, and disease could ruin your lives."

"We feel proud when we survive those challenges," said a school of herring.

"And at least it keeps things interesting. We thought we might die of boredom before," said a troop of mountain gorillas.

Earth's Core smiled up at the life that thrived on the Crust. "Don't you see, my friend? All that change has created something beautiful."

Earth's Crust took a good look at its soil. The parts burned by lava were now lush forests. Each plant and beast was glad to be alive. They made friends and enjoyed good meals. For the first time in millions of years, the Crust felt proud to be their home. It was proud of every bump, crack, and crevice in its rock. All of a sudden, the land started to rumble. The Crust cracked up in an earthquake of laughter. It cried hot geyser tears.

"My sweet Core, I forgive you," sobbed the Crust. "None of this beauty would be possible without you."

Name: ______________________________ Date: ______________

Directions: Read "How Earth Changed." Then, answer the questions.

1. Which description best fits this text?

- (A) a myth about how different landforms were created
- (B) a nonfiction textbook about volcanos
- (C) a how-to book about mountain climbing
- (D) a realistic story about friendship

2. Which is a lesson the Crust learns?

- (A) Change is something you should avoid.
- (B) Change can be hard and also great.
- (C) Only certain things should change.
- (D) Change should be easy for everyone.

3. What does it mean that the Crust *held a grudge*?

- (A) It stayed flat no matter what.
- (B) It held on to the animals.
- (C) It remained mad for a long time.
- (D) It built tall mountains.

4. What is an antonym for *proud*?

- (A) ashamed
- (B) shy
- (C) nervous
- (D) glad

5. Compare and contrast the Crust at the beginning of the story and at the end. Include the Crust's feelings and what it looks like.

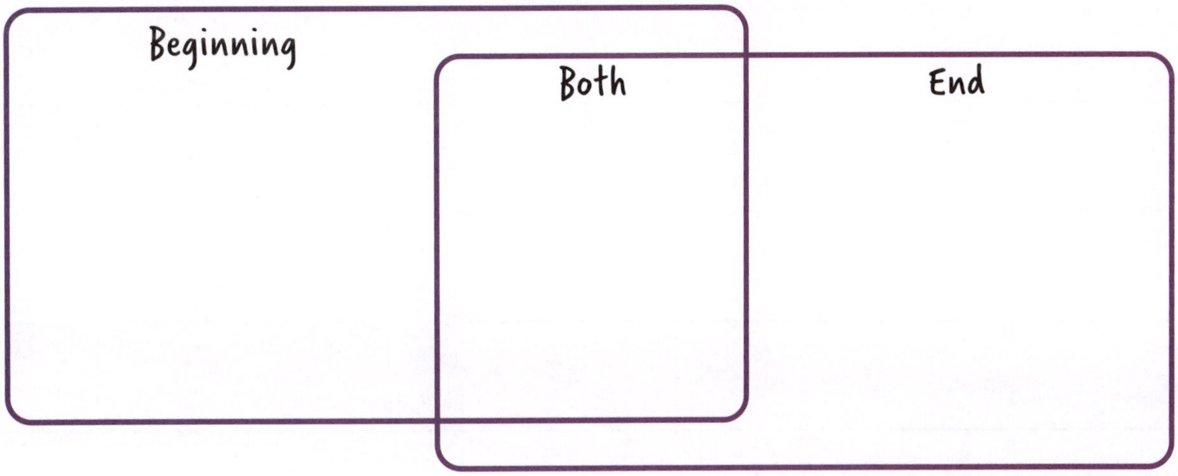

Name: ______________________________ Date: ______________

Directions: Reread the texts from this week. Then, respond to the prompt.

Imagine you are the Core at the very end of the story. Write a journal entry to tell what happened and how you felt. Tell what you think will happen next between you and the Crust.

____

____

____

____

____

____

____

____

____

____

____

____

____

Name: ______________________ Date: ______________

Adventure Ad

Plan your three-day weekend at

Mount Goldfish

- Hike up 50 kilometers (30 miles) of scenic trails! (beginner, intermediate, and advanced trail options available)
- Set up camp at Gold Nugget Campgrounds!
- Catch fish in Pop-Eye River!
- Take a wildlife tour with one of our experienced trail guides!

Tickets go on sale January 1st!

They may sell out quickly. Buy your campground tickets online or over the phone. Wildlife tour tickets are an extra cost. You must bring your own equipment. Call or check our website for prices.

Adventure Awaits!

555-6577

Name: ______________________________ Date: ______________

Directions: Read "Adventure Ad." Then, answer the questions.

1. What is the purpose of this text?
   - (A) to persuade people to visit Mount Goldfish
   - (B) to entertain people with a story about Mount Goldfish
   - (C) to inform people how to hike safely
   - (D) to explain how to spot wildlife on trails

2. Who should not get tickets to stay at Mount Goldfish?
   - (A) people who want to see wildlife
   - (B) people who want to be outdoors
   - (C) people who like to hike
   - (D) people who want to relax indoors

3. Which of the following is a compound word?
   - (A) experienced
   - (B) wildlife
   - (C) tickets
   - (D) advanced

4. Which of the following words has three syllables?
   - (A) experienced
   - (B) campground
   - (C) scenic
   - (D) equipment

5. Which information on the flyer would be most important to you if you wanted to hike at Mount Goldfish? Why?

____

____

____

Name: ______________________________ Date: ____________

Directions: Closely read these texts. Write a dialogue that might occur between mountain climbers and an animal from the story. Think about how they adjust to change.

Close-Reading Texts

Climbing Gear	How Earth Changed
Mountain climbers have to wear special gear that protects them from the snow and cold. They wear a lot of layers that help them stay warm. This includes gloves, hats, and glasses. They also have to use special tools. One tool is an ice axe that helps break up the ice. A regulator is a tool that provides oxygen to climbers. They need this at the tops of peaks where the air is low in oxygen.	Lava kept flowing out of the Core and onto the Crust. It cooled and formed mountains on land and islands in the sea. The land slowly moved. Animals made their homes on these new landforms, and the animals began to change. Some goats moved to tall mountains and changed their hooves into shapes perfect for cliff climbing. Some fish moved to dark caves. They never saw sunlight after that, so they stopped bothering to have eyes.

Name: ______________________________ Date: ______________

Directions: Closely read this text. Then, study "Adventure Ad" from this week. Write what each text is mostly about. Write two ways the texts are similar at the bottom of the chart.

Close-Reading Texts

Climbing Mt. Everest
The Mt. Everest base camps are where climbers begin to climb. These camps are on opposite sides of Mt. Everest. They are also very high. They are more than 16,000 feet (4,877 meters) high. Climbers rest at the base camps. They pack and get their supplies ready before they begin climbing. There are other camps on the way to the peak. It takes a while to reach each camp. Climbers spend time at the camps. This helps them adjust to the elevation.

Climbing Mt. Everest	Adventure Ad

Both

1. ____

____

2. ____

____

Name: ______________________________ Date: ________________

Directions: Think about the texts from this unit. Then, respond to the prompt.

Write to explain why landforms do or do not make Earth a better place. Provide reasons, and support them with facts and details.

* *Landforms are features on Earth's surface. Some examples are mountains, hills, valleys, rivers, and volcanos.*

____

____

____

____

____

____

____

____

____

____

____

Name: ______________________________ Date: ______________

Directions: Imagine Sir Edmund Hillary asks you to design a flyer. He wants it to persuade people to visit Mt. Everest. Give them the details they will need.

Name: ______________________________ Date: ______________

Directions: Read the text, and answer the questions.

As You Read

Think of connections you can make to the text.
Write a ∞ wherever you make connections.

Riptide Warning

Swimming in the ocean is fun. It can also be dangerous. The waves can pull swimmers underwater. A riptide can do this. It is also called a *rip current*. This is a strong channel of water. It can drag people away from the beach. People fight to stay above the surface. Even strong swimmers struggle. Surfers or swimmers should swim parallel to the beach to get out of a rip current. This is very important information to know!

1. Which question does this text try to answer?
   - (A) How do you get sand out of your shoes?
   - (B) How did I get this rip in my pants?
   - (C) Why can swimming in the ocean be dangerous?
   - (D) What do kids learn in swimming lessons?

2. Which word has the same vowel sound as *tide*?
   - (A) film
   - (B) cry
   - (C) rid
   - (D) tidbit

3. What is the definition of *drag* as it is used in this text?
   - (A) moving slowly
   - (B) a nuisance
   - (C) pulling something or someone
   - (D) effort

4. Which word describes the tone of this text?
   - (A) warning
   - (B) sad
   - (C) funny
   - (D) historical

Name: ______________________________ Date: ______________

Directions: Read the text, and answer the questions.

As You Read

Underline information that is new to you. Put stars next to information you already know.

The Truth about Shark Attacks

Small, harmless sharks share the water with swimmers.

Shark attacks are scary to think about when you are at the beach. Hearing a news story of a shark attack may make people think twice about swimming. Swimmers may not want to go in the water, or they may not even want to be on the beach. But the truth is, shark attacks are rare. Often, sharks near shore are on the smaller side, and they are uninterested in humans. If a shark bites a human, it is usually a mistake. A shark may think it is eating a seal. Sharks do not hunt humans. People are not on their menu. But there are ways to be extra careful. It is best to swim in groups and stay near the shore. If you think you see a shark, tell a lifeguard.

1. What does the first sentence say about this text?
   - (A) It is about scary shows on TV.
   - (B) It is about shark attacks.
   - (C) It is about going to the beach.
   - (D) It is about pet sharks.

2. Which two words have the same vowel sound?
   - (A) *seal* and *hunt*
   - (B) *scary* and *rare*
   - (C) *twice* and *think*
   - (D) *beach* and *news*

3. Which of the following words is a synonym for *rare*?
   - (A) each month
   - (B) never
   - (C) always
   - (D) uncommon

4. What type of text would include language similar to what is used in this text?
   - (A) a math textbook
   - (B) a book of animal poems
   - (C) a menu
   - (D) an article about ocean wildlife

Name: ______________________ Date: ______________

Directions: Read the text, and answer the questions.

As You Read

Circle words or phrases that describe beach pollution.

Beach Pollution

Pollution on beaches is troubling. Some of that trash comes from beachgoers. Throwing garbage on the sand pollutes the ocean because the trash makes its way into the water. Some of the trash actually washes up from the ocean. People on boats sometimes drop trash in the water. Pollution can come from many places. People can work together to clean up beaches. They can throw away the trash. This makes beaches nicer places to visit. It helps wildlife there, too!

1. Based on the text, which statement is true?
   - (A) The author wants to teach people about keeping beaches clean.
   - (B) The author thinks beaches are all filthy.
   - (C) The author compares air pollution and water pollution.
   - (D) The author uses facts to tell the history of pollution.

2. Which of these words is the root word of *pollution*?
   - (A) revolution
   - (B) pollute
   - (C) poll
   - (D) Polly

3. What is the main idea of this text?

   ____

   ____

   ____

4. Why might pollution at the beach be harmful to ocean animals?

   ____

   ____

   ____

   ____

Name: ______________________________ Date: ______________

As You Read

Write a ∞ wherever you make connections. Share your connections with a friend or adult.

Being Safe on the Beach

A day at the beach can be wonderful. The coast is quiet and peaceful. The view of the water is very soothing. It can also be quite dangerous. The ocean is very powerful. People need to make safe choices. This will help people avoid injury out in the waves or on the sand.

There is one major way that people can be safe on the coast. They must pay attention to signs and warnings on beaches. Sometimes, flags are flown on beaches. The flags warn people about risky conditions.

Here are the flags that people might see on some beaches:

- A double red flag means the water is closed to the public. The entire beach is closed. People must stay out of the water. This is used for severe weather or currents. Water pollution, lightning, or shark sightings nearby also will get this flag.
- A red flag means there is a high hazard. A high hazard may be high surf and/or strong currents.
- A yellow flag means there is a moderate hazard. A moderate hazard may be strong surf and/or currents.
- A green flag means there are safe conditions. This means that conditions on the beach are safe, but beachgoers should use caution.

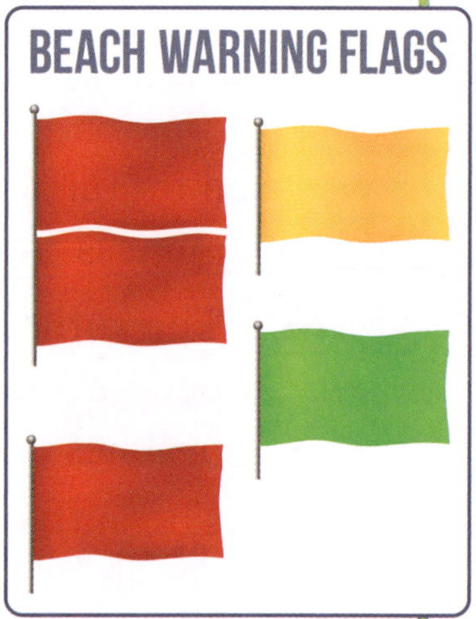

Another way people stay safe is through lifeguards. They watch swimmers and surfers. They keep a close eye on people in the water. They will even watch people on the sand who are near the waves. Lifeguards are trained to help rescue people. They know first aid in case someone gets hurt. They can also call other rescuers to help a person who is in serious trouble.

Not all beaches have lifeguards. Many beaches are public property. This allows people to visit them when they choose. Often, there is no one to stop a person from going into the water. People have to be safe for their own good. A perfect day on the beach is always a safe day on the beach!

Name: ______________________________ Date: ______________

Directions: Read "Being Safe on the Beach." Then, answer the questions.

1. What is the purpose for reading this text?

(A) to be entertained
(B) to be persuaded to avoid the beach
(C) to learn about beach safety
(D) to learn about flags

2. Which statement would the author likely agree with?

(A) People can behave however they want at the beach.
(B) Stay out of the water when lifeguards tell you to do so.
(C) There are no rules at the beach.
(D) Strong swimmers are never in danger.

3. Which statement makes a strong connection to the text?

(A) Our car has hazard lights in case it breaks down.
(B) We fly a flag on the 4th of July.
(C) I stay safe at the beach by sticking close to my family.
(D) I like the colors red and green.

4. Which information in the text is highlighted in a list?

(A) who hangs the flags
(B) where the flags are hung
(C) what the flags mean
(D) the beaches that use this flag system

5. Write three beach safety tips.

Beach Safety Tips

Name: ______________________________ Date: ______________

Directions: Reread "Being Safe on the Beach." Then, respond to the prompt.

There are ways to be safe when you are on the beach. How would you explain the flags to your friends? Write what you would say in words. Then, draw a picture you could show them.

____

____

____

____

____

____

Name: ______________________________ Date: ______________

Directions: Read the text, and answer the questions.

As You Read

Underline words or phrases that tell you about the setting.

Beach Day

One day in June, stormy gray clouds passed over the sea. Jada and her cousin Marlo walked across the beach. They laughed and chased seagulls. They had no clue that a shock was waiting for them in the ocean.

"I'll race you to the water," said Jada. She started to sprint away.

"No fair, Jada," Marlo complained. He rushed after his cousin, but stopped before his feet touched the water. "Come on, you know I'm scared of the ocean. What if a jellyfish stings me?"

"Marlo, you're no fun. I go to the beach all the time. I've never been stung before," scoffed Jada.

"But I just learned about jellyfish in science class. Their tentacles have venom in them!" cried Marlo.

1. What is the relationship between Jada and Marlo?

- (A) They are cousins and friends.
- (B) They are brother and sister.
- (C) They are classmates and friends.
- (D) They are strangers.

2. What is the past tense of *sting*?

- (A) stung
- (B) stang
- (C) stinged
- (D) stinger

3. How many syllables does the word *tentacles* have?

- (A) two
- (B) three
- (C) four
- (D) five

4. How does Marlo feel about the ocean?

- (A) excited
- (B) fearful
- (C) uninterested
- (D) sad

Name: ________________________ Date: ______________

Directions: Read the text, and answer the questions.

As You Read

Underline words or phrases that tell you about the setting.

Dangerous Waters

Jada rolled her eyes. "Jellyfish stings are rare, especially around here. Come play in the water. I'm sure nothing bad will happen," she said.

Marlo crossed his arms and pouted for a moment. Clouds covered the sun, but the summer air still felt hot. The ocean looked cool and refreshing. And his cousin did seem to be having a lot of fun. Finally, Marlo caught up with Jada and splashed her with water.

"OUCH!" yelled Jada.

"I'm not falling for that, Jada. Don't be so dramatic," Marlo scoffed.

"No, really, something hurt my foot—OUCH!" Jada grimaced in pain. She fell backward in the water with a splash.

1. What is the setting of the story?

Ⓐ the middle of the ocean
Ⓑ a boat at sea
Ⓒ a community pool
Ⓓ the beach

2. What does this phrase tell you? *Marlo crossed his arms and pouted for a moment.*

Ⓐ He does not want to go in the water.
Ⓑ He is excited to swim.
Ⓒ He is tired and cold.
Ⓓ He stepped on something.

3. Which suffix could replace *–ing* in *begging* to make a new word?

Ⓐ *–ion*
Ⓑ *–ly*
Ⓒ *–ish*
Ⓓ *–er*

4. Which word is an example of a compound word?

Ⓐ especially
Ⓑ falling
Ⓒ summer
Ⓓ jellyfish

Name: ______________________________ Date: ______________

Directions: Read the text, and answer the questions.

As You Read

Underline words or phrases that describe Jada's actions.

Catch the Culprit

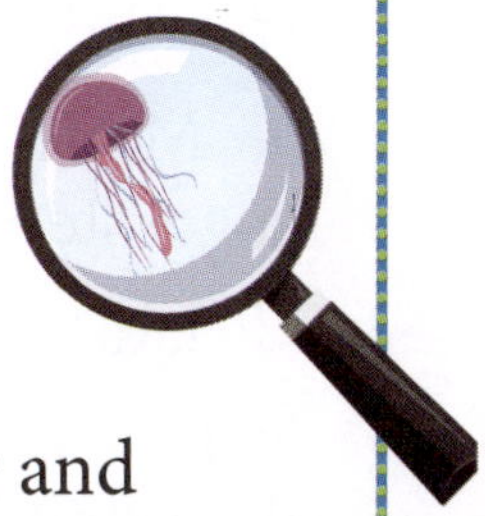

Marlo watched as Jada clutched her left foot. She was still groaning and clenching her teeth. "What happened to you?" Marlo asked.

"I think I stepped on something. It's really painful, like something pinched me," said Jada. She hopped out of the water and took a seat on the sand. Marlo sat next to her and examined the wound.

"See, I told you we would get stung by a jellyfish," Marlo scoffed.

"We can't be sure that the culprit was a jellyfish. I could have been hurt by something else," groaned Jada.

"Then let's figure out what happened," said Marlo.

1. What does the following sentence tell readers? *She was still groaning and clenching her teeth.*
   - (A) Jada feels sick.
   - (B) Jada is in pain.
   - (C) Jada is nervous.
   - (D) Jada is excited.

2. What is the word *culprit* referring to in the text?
   - (A) water
   - (B) falling
   - (C) summer
   - (D) jellyfish

3. Summarize what happened in the text. ______________________________

____

4. Which character do you relate to most? Why?

____

____

Name: ______________________________ Date: ________________

As You Read

Underline descriptive words or phrases that help you visualize the story.

Beach Detectives

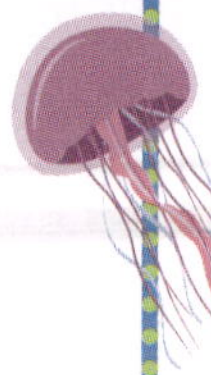

Jada sucked in a deep breath. Her foot still hurt, but talking to Marlo helped take her mind off the pain. "Okay, first, let's think of suspects," she said. "What kinds of things do people step on at the beach?"

Marlo thought for a moment. "There are lots of crabs on the rocks," he suggested.

Jada shook her head. "We aren't near any rocks, though. Maybe I stepped on a broken shell or a piece of glass." She made fists with her hands and squeezed tight. Her foot felt hot. She couldn't think straight.

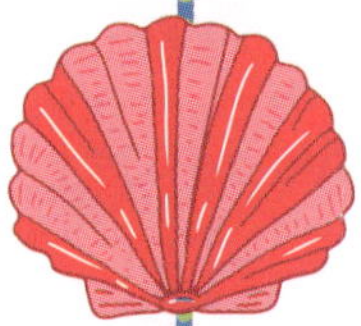

Jada was confused. "If I had stepped on something, it would've hurt the *bottom* of my foot. But it hurts on the *side*." She felt dizzy, so she took another deep breath.

"Okay, then let's look at the wound. We can find evidence to prove what happened," said Marlo.

Jada lifted her left foot and plopped it in Marlo's lap. Both cousins closely examined it. Jada's foot was red and puffy. There was a tiny red circle on the inside. Something gray was sticking out of the wound.

Marlo looked nervous. "That's what stingray wounds look like. Stingrays whip the sides of people's feet with their tail barbs," he said.

"You're only saying that because you're scared of the ocean," Jada said. "I'm sure stingray stings are just as uncommon as jellyfish stings."

"If it hurts more than a normal cut, it could be a sting," Marlo said.

"I'm in a totally normal amount of pain," Jada lied.

"I'm going to find a lifeguard anyway," said Marlo. He returned with a lifeguard a few minutes later.

"That's a stingray barb, all right," said the lifeguard. "I'll pull it out with tweezers, but you should see a doctor right away."

Just like that, Jada and Marlo's beach day was over.

"Sorry I ruined your fun," said Jada.

"You didn't ruin anything," Marlo assured. "It was fun to investigate. Plus, I'm not afraid of the ocean anymore. Even if I get hurt, I know I can be just as brave as you."

Jada grinned and said, "Next time, we'll see who can swim the farthest."

Name: ______________________________ Date: ________________

Directions: Read "Beach Detectives." Then, answer the questions.

1. What is the cause of Jada's wound?
   - (A) a jellyfish
   - (B) coral
   - (C) a sharp rock
   - (D) a stingray

2. Where is Jada's wound?
   - (A) on the bottom of her foot
   - (B) on the side of her foot
   - (C) on her ankle
   - (D) on her toe

3. What is the base word of *scraped*?
   - (A) scrap
   - (B) *–ed*
   - (C) scrape
   - (D) scrapping

4. What genre of text is this?
   - (A) historical fiction
   - (B) nonfiction
   - (C) fantasy
   - (D) realistic fiction

5. Write details about the story elements of the text.

Beach Detectives	
Characters	Setting
Problem	Solution

Name: ______________________________ Date: ________________

Directions: Reread "Beach Detectives." Then, respond to the prompt.

Write a book review for this story. Share your opinions of the story. Would you recommend it to someone else? Why or why not?

Name: ______________________________ Date: ________________

Summer Job

Looking for a summer job? Chester City Pool needs you.

Apply to be a lifeguard!

To apply, you must be:

- at least 15 years old
- certified in first aid and CPR
- willing and able to pass an advanced swim test

Applications are due **May 25.**

Mail the attached form to:

56 Poolside Drive, Chester City, MD 90021

Questions? Call
555-200-3797

Name: ______________________________ Date: ______________

Directions: Read "Summer Job." Then, answer the questions.

1. What job is being advertised?

Ⓐ server
Ⓑ store clerk
Ⓒ lifeguard
Ⓓ cashier

2. When are applications due?

Ⓐ May 25
Ⓑ March 15
Ⓒ May 1
Ⓓ March 30

3. How many syllables are in the word *applications*?

Ⓐ two syllables
Ⓑ three syllables
Ⓒ four syllables
Ⓓ five syllables

4. Which words have the same vowel sound?

Ⓐ aid and able
Ⓑ swim and life
Ⓒ first and city
Ⓓ pool and form

5. Which information on the job posting do you think would be most important if you wanted to apply? Why?

____

____

____

____

____

____

____

____

Name: ______________________________ Date: ________________

Directions: Closely read these texts. Then, study the job posting on page 41. Write about the author's purpose(s) for each of these texts.

Close-Reading Texts

Being Safe on the Beach	Beach Detectives
• A red flag means there is a high hazard. A high hazard may be high surf and/or strong currents. • A yellow flag means there is a moderate hazard. A moderate hazard may be strong surf and/or currents. • A green flag means there are safe conditions. This means that conditions on the beach are safe, but beachgoers should use caution.	Marlo looked nervous. "That's what stingray wounds look like. Stingrays whip the sides of people's feet with their tail barbs," he said. "You're only saying that because you're scared of the ocean," Jada said. "I'm sure stingray stings are just as uncommon as jellyfish stings." "If it hurts more than a normal cut, it could be a sting," Marlo said. "I'm in a totally normal amount of pain," Jada lied. "I'm going to find a lifeguard anyway," said Marlo.

Text	Author's Purpose(s)
Being Safe on the Beach	
Beach Detectives	
Summer Job	

Name: ______________________________ Date: ______________

Directions: Closely read these texts. Compare and contrast their topics, genres, purposes, and anything else you notice.

Close-Reading Texts

Beach Detectives	Being Safe on the Beach
"I'm in a totally normal amount of pain," Jada lied. "I'm going to find a lifeguard anyway," said Marlo. He returned with a lifeguard a few minutes later. "That's a stingray barb, all right," said the lifeguard. "I'll pull it out with tweezers, but you should see a doctor right away."	Another way people stay safe is through lifeguards. They watch swimmers and surfers. They keep a close eye on people in the water. They will even watch people on the sand who are near the waves. Lifeguards are trained to help rescue people. They know first aid in case someone gets hurt. They can also call other rescuers to help a person who is in serious trouble.

Beach Detectives	Being Safe on the Beach

Both

Name: ______________________ Date: ______________

Directions: Think about the texts from this unit. Then, respond to the prompt.

Write a story that takes place at the beach. It should have something to do with being safe at the beach. Make sure it has a beginning, middle, and end.

____

____

____

____

____

____

____

____

____

____

____

____

Name: ______________________ Date: ____________

Directions: Think of some summer jobs you might want when you are in high school. Choose one. Create a job posting for the job. Tell what the job is about. Give details about how to apply.

Name: ______________________ Date: ______________

Directions: Read the text, and answer the questions.

As You Read

Put stars next to words that describe Rome and/or its buildings.

Ancient Ruins

Rome has many famous buildings. Many are from ancient times. The Forum is one of the most famous places. At one time, it was the center of Rome. Tourists can still visit the Forum and see the ruins. The ruins stand amid the modern city. The Pantheon is another famous building. It still stands in Rome. It was a temple dedicated to the gods.

1. What is the text about?
   - (A) Roman gods
   - (B) buildings in Rome
   - (C) modern cities
   - (D) centers of cities

2. Which word has the same vowel sound as *Rome*?
   - (A) most
   - (B) one
   - (C) ruins
   - (D) modern

3. What is the definition of *amid*?
   - (A) within
   - (B) next to
   - (C) in front of
   - (D) far

4. Which word describes the tone of this text?
   - (A) factual
   - (B) silly
   - (C) funny
   - (D) mysterious

Name: ______________________ Date: ______________

Directions: Read the text, and answer the questions.

As You Read

Underline information that you find surprising or interesting.

Roman Calendar

The ancient Romans invented many things that are used today. One thing that came from Roman times is our calendar system. The first calendar in Rome was based on lunar months. That means it was based on the phases of the moon. It confused people. Roman leader Julius Caesar asked for a new one. It had 365 days in a year. There is an extra day in February every four years. It is known as a *leap day*. We still use this calendar system.

1. What does the first sentence say about this text?

- (A) It is about ancient Roman inventions.
- (B) It is about how to be an inventor.
- (C) It is about using something for a long time.
- (D) It is about visiting Rome.

2. Why did Caesar ask for a new calendar?

- (A) He wanted a calendar named after him.
- (B) The old calendar was too simple.
- (C) The old calendar was confusing.
- (D) He wanted the seasons to be different.

3. Which word has the same root word as *invented*?

- (A) vent
- (B) inventor
- (C) invite
- (D) provide

4. What other type of text is most similar to this text?

- (A) a history book
- (B) a book of poetry
- (C) a menu
- (D) a thank-you note

Name: ______________________________ Date: ______________

Directions: Read the text, and answer the questions.

As You Read

Put stars next to information about water in ancient Rome.

Water in Ancient Rome

Water was important to ancient Romans. Rome got very hot. People needed water to stay cool. Many Romans also liked to be clean. They used clean water to bathe. Romans built a good water system. They built aqueducts. These carried water to different places in the city. Some homes even had fresh water inside. Towns were often built near clean water supplies.

ancient Roman aqueduct

1. Which statement about the text is true?

- (A) The author uses facts to teach about how to bathe.
- (B) The author uses funny statements to make people laugh about clean water.
- (C) The author compares baths and showers.
- (D) The author uses facts to teach about ancient Rome's water supply.

2. Which index entry would help a reader find this information?

- (A) water in ancient Rome
- (B) town names
- (C) city government
- (D) all of the above

3. Describe aqueducts.

____

____

____

4. Would you have wanted to live in ancient Rome? Why or why not?

____

____

____

____

Name: ______________________ Date: ______________

As You Read

Underline positive things about Julius Caesar.
Circle negative things about him.

Julius Caesar

Julius Caesar is an important person in history. He was a leader during ancient times. He lived in ancient Rome. Caesar was born in 100 BCE. He grew up in a simple home. His family belonged to an old Roman family. They were not rich or poor.

Most boys like Caesar did not go to school. They had tutors. Caesar had a tutor, too. He learned a lot from his tutor. He learned to read and write Latin. He also became a good public speaker. These skills would help him later in life.

Caesar fell in love with a girl named Cornelia. They got married. They had a daughter. They all lived together in Rome.

Caesar rose to power as time went on. He was given important jobs. Caesar had joined the army at a young age. He quickly became a leader in the army. The troops liked him a lot. People respected him. They also started to pay attention to him. He won many battles for Rome. The Roman army was very powerful. Having the respect of that army was a very big deal.

In Rome, the leaders were in trouble. The republic was in shambles. Leaders were arguing. Finally, the Senate was forced to change. Three men took over as leaders. One was Caesar. Soon after, Caesar fought for all the power. He took over as the only leader of Rome. He made himself a dictator. This made people upset. Romans did not want a king. A dictator was too much like a king. They did not want Caesar to change their lives too much. Some members of the Senate decided to kill Caesar. They stabbed him to death. The day he was killed is known as the Ides of March.

Many men ruled over Rome after Caesar. Some were good leaders. Some were not. The Roman Empire changed a lot over the years. But Caesar will always be remembered. He was one of Rome's important leaders.

Name: ______________________ Date: ______________

Directions: Read "Julius Caesar." Then, answer the questions.

1. What is the author's purpose for readers?

Ⓐ to read a biography of Julius Caesar
Ⓑ to read a story about Roman life
Ⓒ to learn about Roman army strategies
Ⓓ to learn how to be a good leader

2. Who did Caesar fight for power?

Ⓐ Cornelia
Ⓑ his tutor
Ⓒ the Roman army
Ⓓ the two other leaders

3. What alternative title reflects the main idea of the text?

Ⓐ The Leader of a Great Army
Ⓑ Successes and Struggles of Julius Caesar
Ⓒ A Smart Marriage
Ⓓ Betrayed by the Man

4. What mistake led to Caesar's death?

Ⓐ He did not know how to lead.
Ⓑ He was not smart enough.
Ⓒ The army did not respect him.
Ⓓ He tried to have too much power.

5. Write five things that happened in Caesar's life in chronological order.

Life Events of Julius Caesar	
1	
2	
3	
4	
5	

Name: ______________________________ Date: ______________

Directions: Reread "Julius Caesar." Then, respond to the prompt.

Julius Caesar had a life full of ups and downs. Do you think he was a smart leader? Why or why not?

Name: ______________________________ Date: ______________

Directions: Read the text, and answer the questions.

As You Read

Underline words or phrases that describe the setting.

A Roman Morning

Each morning, Tullia woke up long before the sun rose. She lived right next to a crowded cobblestone street. Horses' hooves clopped on the road. Chariot wheels clacked against the stones. Shopkeepers rushed to open their shops. People had to yell to be heard over the din. To top it all off, a blacksmith worked nearby. The sound of metal clanged all day. Tullia yawned and stretched. She put on a clean tunic and drank a cup of water. It was time for another noisy day in Rome.

1. Which adjectives best describe the setting?

- Ⓐ hot and humid
- Ⓑ busy and noisy
- Ⓒ quiet and calm
- Ⓓ cold and quiet

2. What is the main character's name?

- Ⓐ Tullia
- Ⓑ Rome
- Ⓒ Chariot
- Ⓓ Julius

3. What is the definition of *din*?

- Ⓐ loud noise
- Ⓑ large horse
- Ⓒ early morning
- Ⓓ metal

4. What type of material does a blacksmith work with?

- Ⓐ wood
- Ⓑ cobblestone
- Ⓒ metal
- Ⓓ cloth

Name: ______________________________ Date: ______________

Directions: Read the text, and answer the questions.

As You Read

Put a ? next to anything that is confusing, such as unfamiliar words.

To the Market

"Tullia, please go to the market. I need a new set of sewing needles. I've lost my old ones, and your father needs a new tunic," said Tullia's mother. Her mother was wide awake, too. She was already busy weaving wool. Her fingers flew across the loom.

Tullia watched how fast her mother moved. "Yes, Mother," she said. "May I help you weave when I get back?"

"Of course, dear. Now, hurry along," said Tullia's mother.

1. Why does Tullia need to go to the market?

- (A) to get sewing needles
- (B) to buy a tunic
- (C) to get a jug of water
- (D) to buy some bread

2. What does the author mean by *Her fingers flew across the loom*?

- (A) She weaved very quickly.
- (B) She made mistakes as she weaved.
- (C) She rubbed her fingers up and down.
- (D) She hit the loom with her fingers.

3. Which word is spelled correctly?

- (A) weaveing
- (B) weaving
- (C) weeving
- (D) weiveing

4. What is the root word in *sewing*?

- (A) wing
- (B) sew
- (C) *–ing*
- (D) so

Name: ______________________ Date: ______________

Directions: Read the text, and answer the questions.

As You Read

Underline words or phrases that describe the setting.

A Quieter Future

Tullia raced down the street. She made sure not to trip on the uneven stones. As she ran, she heard bits and pieces of people talking.

"Buy fresh leeks and onions here!" yelled a merchant.

"Portable ovens, half price! Take your oven with you wherever you go!" yelled another.

"I can't wait for Julius Caesar's new law to take effect. The streets will be much quieter," a woman said. Tullia slowed down, and her ears perked up.

"I'm excited, too," a man replied. "No chariots during the day! That sounds like a dream."

Tullia gasped in disbelief. *I hope that law will take effect soon*, she thought. *Maybe I will be able to sleep in past sunrise!*

1. What is the setting?

- (A) the streets of ancient Rome
- (B) the streets of Rome today
- (C) inside a chariot
- (D) Julius Caesar's house

2. Why are some of the words in the text in italics?

- (A) to show what Tullia says
- (B) to show what Tullia thinks
- (C) to show when other people talk
- (D) to show a strong emotion

3. What is the new law people talk about in the text?

____

____

4. What is one question you would ask Tullia if you could?

____

____

____

Name: ______________________ Date: ____________

As You Read

Underline words or phrases that describe sounds in the story.

The Sounds of Rome

Clang! Once again, Tullia woke up before dawn. The blacksmith still clanged his metal tools. The shopkeepers still talked loudly. But the clip and clop of chariot traffic was gone! Julius Caesar's law had passed. Horses could not pull chariots through the streets. Not in the daytime, at least. Tullia rubbed her eyes and rolled over on her mat. With less noise, she could sleep a bit longer. She finally got out of bed when the sun shone bright in her eyes.

Tullia went to the market again. Her leather sandals slapped against the cobblestone street. *What a strange sound*, Tullia thought. Just yesterday, she couldn't hear her footsteps at all. She was amazed by all she heard. Ravens cawed and flapped their wings. Tree leaves rustled. Babies cried, and parents shushed them. Tullia noticed how slowly her feet moved. When the street was full of traffic, she would run as fast as she could. She hated the crowds and the noise. This time, she enjoyed her stroll.

The rest of Tullia's day was just as quiet. Once her chores were done, she went to the bath house. Everyone in Rome went there to wash up. They would talk to each other about their days. Today, people spoke in soft, calm voices as they bathed. Tullia noticed that most of them were smiling. They all seemed well rested and relaxed. Tullia felt the same.

In the evening, all the people of Rome watched the sun go down. They settled into their beds. "Sleep well, my sweet," said Tullia's mother.

"I'm sure I will," said Tullia. She closed her eyes, and…

Clack-clack-clack clip-clop-clip-clop!

Tullia groaned. All the people of Rome groaned. From now on, chariots would only cross the streets at night.

Name: ______________________________ Date: ______________

Directions: Read "The Sounds of Rome." Then, answer the questions.

1. What genre of text is this?

Ⓐ poetry
Ⓑ nonfiction
Ⓒ fantasy
Ⓓ historical fiction

2. What does Tullia do after she does her chores?

Ⓐ She goes to the market.
Ⓑ She weaves a new tunic.
Ⓒ She goes to the bath house.
Ⓓ She goes to sleep.

3. Which words have the same vowel sound?

Ⓐ *groan* and *Rome*
Ⓑ *soft* and *groan*
Ⓒ *chores* and *done*
Ⓓ *to* and *clop*

4. *Clang!* is an example of ______.

Ⓐ onomatopoeia
Ⓑ simile
Ⓒ metaphor
Ⓓ hyperbole

5. Write an effect for each cause.

Cause	Effect
1. Tullia walks slowly through the market.	
2. Julius Caesar's law passed.	
3. Chariots cross the streets at night.	

Name: ______________________ Date: ______________

Directions: Reread "The Sounds of Rome." Then, respond to the prompt.

You are a character in the story. Would you prefer a law that said no chariots during the day or no chariots at night? Explain your thinking.

Name: ______________________________ Date: ______________

Grandma's Best Garum

Here is a recipe for the most popular fish sauce in Rome. First, make a brine from water and many grains of salt. If an egg is placed in the brine, the egg should float. If the egg sinks, add more salt. Next, place two pounds of whole mackerel fish in the brine. Season the fish with a large spoonful of oregano. Pour in a few ounces of grape syrup. Boil the mixture for at least 30 minutes, but no more than one hour. Be sure to break the mackerel into small pieces. Finally, let the mixture cool down. Strain it through a sieve until only liquid is left. Pour the garum into a tall clay pot. Use this to add flavor to any meat or vegetable dish.

Name: ______________________________ Date: ________________

Directions: Read "Grandma's Best Garum." Then, answer the questions.

1. What does the text say to do first?

- (A) season the fish
- (B) make a brine
- (C) break the mackerel into small pieces
- (D) let the mixture cool

2. Where would this text most likely be found?

- (A) a dictionary
- (B) a book of poetry
- (C) a cookbook
- (D) a science textbook

3. What is garum used for?

- (A) to sprinkle on pizza or pasta
- (B) to pour over ice cream for dessert
- (C) to mix in a salad
- (D) to add flavor to meat or vegetable dishes

4. What is mackerel?

- (A) a fish
- (B) a vegetable
- (C) a bowl
- (D) a sauce

5. Would you want to try to make this recipe? Why or why not?

____

____

____

____

Name: ______________________ Date: ______________

Directions: Closely read these texts. Look for words or phrases that describe life in ancient Rome. Circle them. Write the words in the chart.

Close-Reading Texts

Water in Ancient Rome	A Roman Morning
Water was important to ancient Romans. Rome got very hot. People needed water to stay cool. Many Romans also liked to be clean. They used clean water to bathe. Romans built a good water system. They built aqueducts. These carried water to different places in the city. Some homes even had fresh water inside. Towns were often built near clean water supplies.	Each morning, Tullia woke up long before the sun rose. She lived right next to a crowded cobblestone street. Horses' hooves clopped on the road. Chariot wheels clacked against the stones. Shopkeepers rushed to open their shops. People had to yell to be heard over the din. To top it all off, a blacksmith worked nearby. The sound of metal clanged all day. Tullia yawned and stretched. She put on a clean tunic and drank a cup of water. It was time for another noisy day in Rome.

Text	Words and Phrases about Ancient Rome
Water in Ancient Rome	
A Roman Morning	

Name: ______________________ Date: ______________

Directions: Closely read these texts. Then, compare and contrast Julius Caesar with the character Tullia.

Close-Reading Texts

Julius Caesar	To the Market
Julius Caesar is an important person in history. He was a leader during ancient times. He lived in ancient Rome. Caesar was born in 100 BCE. He grew up in a simple home. His family belonged to an old Roman family. They were not rich or poor. Most boys like Caesar did not go to school. They had tutors. Caesar had a tutor, too. He learned a lot from his tutor. He learned to read and write Latin. He also became a good public speaker. These skills would help him later in life.	"Tullia, please go to the market. I need a new set of sewing needles. I've lost my old ones, and your father needs a new tunic," said Tullia's mother. Her mother was wide awake, too. She was already busy weaving wool. Her fingers flew across the loom. Tullia watched how fast her mother moved. "Yes, Mother," she said. "May I help you weave when I get back?"

Julius Caesar	Tullia
Both	

Name: ______________________________ Date: ______________

Directions: Think about the texts from this unit. Then, respond to the prompt.

Imagine you live in ancient Rome. Write a diary entry. Describe your day and what is going on in your life.

____

____

____

____

____

____

____

____

____

____

____

____

____

Name: ______________________________ Date: ______________

Directions: Think of a snack or meal you like to eat. Describe how to make it. It does not have to be something you cook. Draw pictures to help readers understand how to make it.

How to Make ______________________

____

____

____

____

____

____

____

Name: ______________________ Date: ______________

Directions: Read the text, and answer the questions.

As You Read

Underline information that is new to you. Put a star next to information you already know.

Soccer or Football?

Is soccer the same as football, or are they two different sports? Well, it depends on whom you ask. Americans know soccer as a kicking game played with goals. Football involves tackling. Touchdowns are scored instead of goals. Other countries have different names for these games. Some call the kicking game football instead of soccer. It can be very confusing!

1. What do you score in soccer?
   - (A) a basket
   - (B) a goal
   - (C) a touchdown
   - (D) a corner kick

2. Which word has the same vowel sound as *games*?
   - (A) gander
   - (B) gash
   - (C) time
   - (D) aim

3. What is an antonym of the word *confusing*?
   - (A) quick
   - (B) dark
   - (C) obvious
   - (D) difficult

4. What does the phrase *it depends on whom you ask* mean in the text?
   - (A) Some people will not know the answer.
   - (B) Some people will be rude if you ask them.
   - (C) You will get different answers from different people.
   - (D) People agree on the answer.

Name: ______________________ Date: ____________

Directions: Read the text, and answer the questions.

As You Read

Underline information that is new to you. Put a star next to information you already know.

Soccer Rules

The offside rule in soccer is good to know. A player can be called offside. This happens when a player stands closer to the opponent's goal than the ball and a defending player. A player cannot receive a pass next to the goal and the goalie. This rule makes the soccer game fair. It keeps players from hanging out by the goal and waiting for a pass.

1. Which statement summarizes the text?
   - (A) This text explains how referees make calls.
   - (B) This text explains how kids learn soccer skills.
   - (C) This text explains what rules are easily broken during a soccer game.
   - (D) This text explains what the offside rule is.

2. Which two words have the same vowel sound?
   - (A) *good* and *know*
   - (B) *not* and *goal*
   - (C) *keeps* and *receives*
   - (D) *ball* and *pass*

3. Which word is an antonym of *opponent*?
   - (A) friend
   - (B) teammate
   - (C) coach
   - (D) teacher

4. What does the phrase *makes the soccer game fair* mean in the text?
   - (A) slowing people down
   - (B) prevents people from cheating
   - (C) makes the game fun to watch
   - (D) keeps coaches happy

Name: ______________________ Date: ______________

Directions: Read the text, and answer the questions.

As You Read

Underline information that is new to you. Put a star next to information you already know.

The World Cup

Where can a fan watch the best male soccer players in the world? At the World Cup, of course. The World Cup is the biggest soccer competition in the world. Billions of people watch the final game on TV. It happens every four years. There are 32 teams that compete for the winning title. Brazil has won the most titles, winning five times.

World Cup trophy

1. The phrase *At the World Cup, of course* shows that the author _____.
   - (A) dislikes the World Cup
   - (B) thinks most readers know about the World Cup
   - (C) is going to the World Cup
   - (D) is a soccer player on a World Cup team

2. Which two words have the same root word?
   - (A) *compete* and *competition*
   - (B) *male* and *most*
   - (C) *team* and *title*
   - (D) *compete* and *course*

3. What is the main idea of this text?

   ____

   ____

4. Would you like to go to a World Cup soccer game? Why or why not?

   ____

   ____

   ____

   ____

Name: ______________________ Date: ____________

As You Read

Underline information that is new or interesting.

Kicking It with Beckham

Many kids grow up wanting to become famous athletes. David Beckham did. Many people who know him say that he was born to be a soccer player. He has loved the game from a very young age.

Beckham grew up in England. He lived a simple life. He played soccer constantly as a young boy. He worked hard on his skills. It has always been the biggest part of his life. He played his first professional game in 1992 as a young man. He was only 17 years old. He played for the Manchester United team.

Beckham quickly became a fan favorite. He played midfield and helped to move the ball for his team. He got a lot of attention for one goal he made in 1996. During a game, he noticed a goalie who was out of the goal. He kicked a goal from the halfway line of the field. He made it! Many people started to notice Beckham after this play. He continued to work hard. Beckham helped his team win many games. He was also in the running for the World Player of the Year. People enjoyed watching him play.

In 2003, he was transferred to the Real Madrid team in Spain. He began to earn a lot of money for his smart footwork! His life truly became a rags-to-riches story. Beckham came from a simple life to earn millions of dollars playing soccer.

Beckham played with the Los Angeles Galaxy team from 2007 to 2012. He dealt with several injuries in his career and missed some games. In 2013, he retired from professional soccer. Yet David Beckham remains one of the great soccer players in the world. In 2021, he was inducted into England's Premier League Hall of Fame.

Name: ______________________________ Date: ________________

Directions: Read "Kicking It with Beckham." Then, answer the questions.

1. Which sentence shares the author's opinion?

Ⓐ People enjoyed watching him play.
Ⓑ David Beckham quickly became a fan favorite.
Ⓒ Yet Beckham remains one of the great soccer players in the world.
Ⓓ He has loved the game from a very young age.

2. How many professional soccer teams are mentioned?

Ⓐ one team
Ⓑ two teams
Ⓒ three teams
Ⓓ four teams

3. Which statement shows a strong connection to this text?

Ⓐ This reminds me of being a fan of a movie star.
Ⓑ This reminds me of reading a story like "Hansel and Gretel."
Ⓒ This reminds me of playing at the beach.
Ⓓ This reminds me of working hard to learn how to play tennis.

4. What is the most important point made in the text about Beckham's life?

Ⓐ He was only 17 when he became a professional soccer player.
Ⓑ He worked hard, and his life story went from rags to riches.
Ⓒ He played for three different teams.
Ⓓ He grew up in England.

5. Write four major events in Beckham's career. Write them in the order they occurred.

Event 1	Beckham played for the Manchester United team.
Event 2	
Event 3	
Event 4	

Name: ______________________________ Date: ______________

Directions: Reread "Kicking It with Beckham." Then, respond to the prompt.

Write a letter to David Beckham. Tell him what you found most interesting about him. Ask him questions you have about his life and career. You can share a connection. For example: "Do you have a sport or hobby you love?" Does Beckham remind you of anyone? Tell him about it!

________________________,

____

____

____

____

____

____

____

____

____

________________________,

____

Name: ______________________________ Date: ______________

Directions: Read the text, and answer the questions.

As You Read

Think of connections you can make to the text.
Write a ∞ wherever you make connections.

How to Be a Star

I read an article last Monday. It was about a basketball star. I wanted to know his secret. How did he become an amazing athlete? I wanted to improve, too. I have been working on my skills in soccer. I learned that the athlete worked hard. He was serious. He believed in himself. This helped me focus on my own strengths. I knew I had to work hard during soccer practice, especially since I had a big game coming up.

1. What is this text about?

- (A) rooting for an athlete
- (B) basketball players wearing glasses to see the ball
- (C) the importance of believing in yourself and working hard
- (D) watching a basketball game and learning the rules

2. Which suffix could be added to the root word *work* to make a new word?

- (A) *–es*
- (B) *–ly*
- (C) *–tion*
- (D) *–er*

3. What is the definition of *focus*?

- (A) improve
- (B) pay close attention to
- (C) support
- (D) move quickly

4. Which phrase is an example of alliteration?

- (A) knows his secret
- (B) the athlete worked hard
- (C) amazing athlete
- (D) focus on her own

Name: ______________________________ Date: ______________

Directions: Read the text, and answer the questions.

As You Read

Write a ∞ wherever you make connections to the text.

Watching Soccer Together

After soccer practice last Wednesday, my friend Josie came over. We watched a soccer game on TV. Manchester United was playing Real Madrid. We had different opinions about the game. I wanted Real Madrid to win. Josie did not care who won. She wanted it to be a good game with lots of action.

Manchester United won, 3–0. We shared our thoughts about the game. Josie wanted the score of the game to be closer. She thought that made games more exciting. I just wished my team had won. It was still a good game. We had fun watching it together.

1. Which word means a *personal view*?
   - (A) opinion
   - (B) news
   - (C) poetry
   - (D) genre

2. Which word is the root word in *shared*?
   - (A) hare
   - (B) share
   - (C) hared
   - (D) are

3. Which could be a strong title for this text?
   - (A) Different Opinions
   - (B) Bad Games
   - (C) Winners or Action?
   - (D) Best Game Ever

4. How could you describe the opinions of the two main characters?
   - (A) The narrator and Josie cannot agree on what to watch.
   - (B) The narrator and Josie agree on who should have won the game.
   - (C) The narrator and Josie have different opinions, but they both hated the game.
   - (D) The narrator and Josie have different opinions, but they both liked the game.

Name: ______________________ Date: ______________

Directions: Read the text, and answer the questions.

As You Read

Write a ∞ wherever you make connections to the text.

The Big Game

Saturday could not come soon enough. My soccer team had a big game. I had done really well in practice all week, and I was confident we would win. But first, I had to get through Friday at school. That meant I had to get through math class.

"It's testing day today," my math teacher reminded us as we walked in the door. "Remember that the test is timed. I will keep an eye on the clock. When the bell rings, the test will be over. You have 45 minutes to answer the questions."

I took a deep breath and opened my test book. I really did not want to hear the bell until I was finished!

1. What is the setting?

- Ⓐ a classroom
- Ⓑ a bookstore
- Ⓒ the playground
- Ⓓ home

2. What is the tone of the last sentence?

- Ⓐ hopeless
- Ⓑ casual
- Ⓒ nervous
- Ⓓ thankful

3. Describe a picture that would tell the reader more about this text.

____

4. Explain a connection you can make to this text.

____

____

Name: ______________________ Date: ____________

As You Read

Write a ∞ wherever you make connections to the text.

Taking the Shot

I have always hated games that come down to the final seconds. It makes me too anxious to know that anything can happen.

So, you can imagine how it felt to have about one minute left on the clock during our soccer game last weekend. Our team was playing the Devils, and the score was 4–3. We were down by one goal and hoping to score before the final whistle. If we could tie the game, the two teams would play in overtime for a winner.

This was an important game. It was the last one of the season. The winner of this game would move on to the city championship.

I was playing the forward position on that day and was running the ball up the field with my friend, Josie. We were passing it back and forth and making a lot of progress. We had practiced this all week. I could hear the crowd cheering and thought I even heard my mom yell my name. I was very focused, so all I could do was keep my eye on the ball and watch the goal. I was looking for any opening to make a shot. I knew the goalie was a bit slow, so if she had to run after a ball quickly, it might just slip past her. It was my only hope.

In an instant, I saw my chance. I could see a line straight through to the net. I was sure that the ball would sail right past the goalie. I planted my left foot and aimed my right leg toward the goal. I kicked that ball with all my might. I watched the ball go right into the goalie's hands. Then, I heard the whistle.

The game was over. I had never felt such disappointment before. I felt like I let my team down. But my coach gave me a high five and told me I had a good game. My teammates kept saying things like, "Nice try!" or, "Next time you'll make it!" But I was still sad. I wanted to win so badly, but I missed the shot. I think I would have felt worse if I did not take the shot at all, though. I guess I know what I'll be working on in practice.

Name: ______________________ Date: ____________

Directions: Read "Taking the Shot." Then, answer the questions.

1. Which statement is true about the narrator?

Ⓐ She does not like close games.
Ⓑ She is a horrible soccer player.
Ⓒ She does not want to go to the city championship.
Ⓓ She does not trust Alex.

2. Who would most likely relate to the narrator's experience?

Ⓐ a goalie who catches a ball
Ⓑ a teacher who forgets to give a spelling test
Ⓒ a chef who burns a meal and has to start over
Ⓓ a gymnast who falls and causes her team to lose

3. What is the author's opinion?

Ⓐ It is better to be a team player than to hog the ball.
Ⓑ Losing a game is the worst thing to ever happen.
Ⓒ Losing an important game can be very disappointing.
Ⓓ Soccer is too competitive.

4. Which word describes the ending of the story?

Ⓐ mysterious
Ⓑ exciting
Ⓒ happy
Ⓓ disappointing

5. Describe the beginning, middle, and end of the story.

Beginning	Middle	End

Name: ______________________________ Date: ______________

Directions: Reread "Taking the Shot." Then, respond to the prompt.

Write your own version of how the story ends. Add to or change it to make it different.

In an instant, I saw my chance. ______________________________

Name: ______________________________ Date: ________________

Soccer Camp Flyer

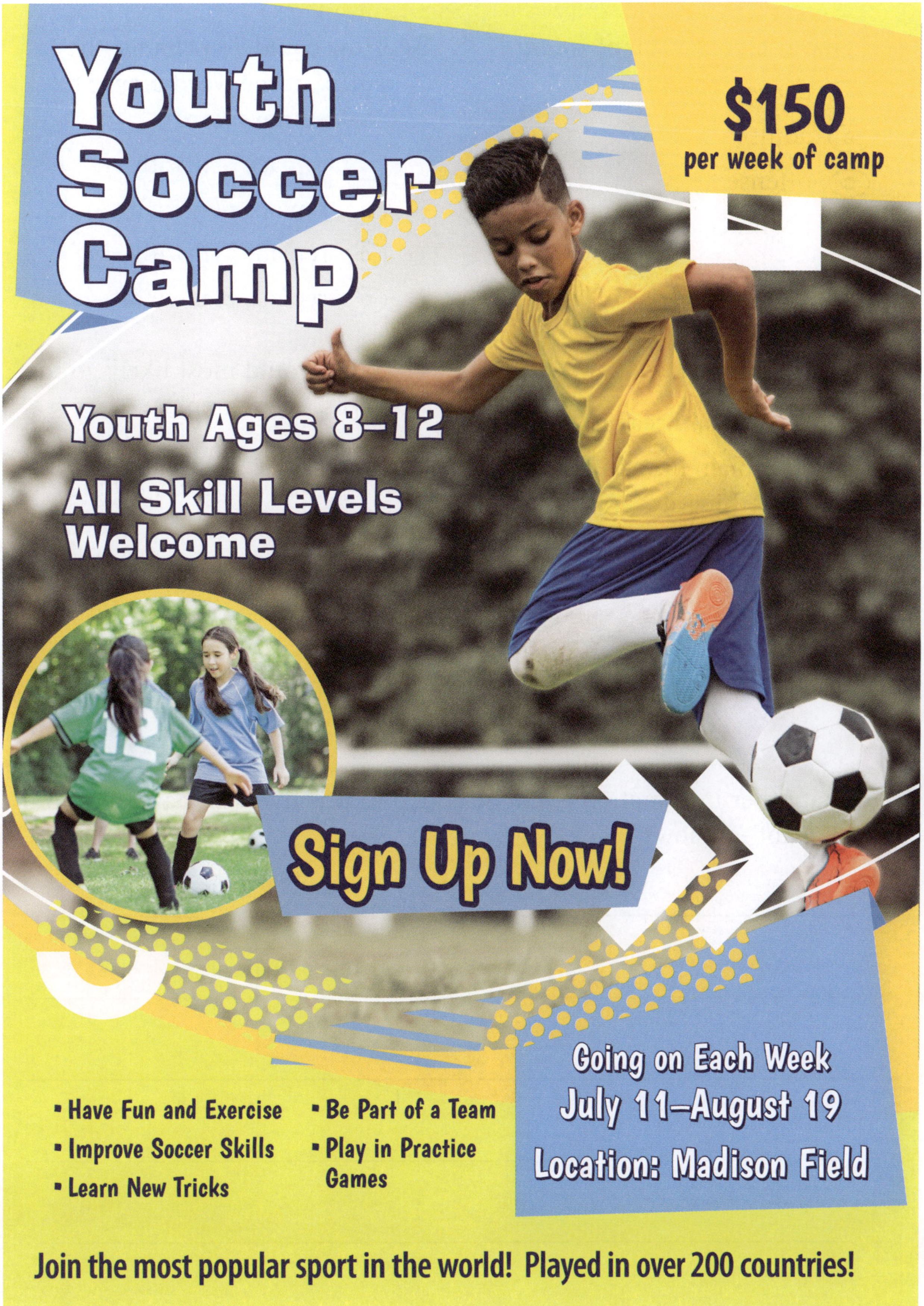

Name: ______________________ Date: ____________

Directions: Read "Soccer Camp Flyer." Then, answer the questions.

1. What is an antonym of *youth*?

Ⓐ coach
Ⓑ adult
Ⓒ offense
Ⓓ beginner

2. What is the purpose of this flyer?

Ⓐ to advertise something
Ⓑ to entertain readers
Ⓒ to explain how to do something
Ⓓ to share an opinion

3. How could you change the suffix in the word *played* to make a new word?

Ⓐ replace –*ed* with –*ly*
Ⓑ replace *play*– with *kick*–
Ⓒ replace –*ed* with –*ing*
Ⓓ replace *play*– with –*er*

4. Who would most likely go to this soccer camp?

Ⓐ a high school soccer player who wants to play in college
Ⓑ a professional soccer player
Ⓒ a nine-year-old who loves soccer
Ⓓ a nine-year-old who wants to get better at basketball

5. What other information could be added to this flyer? What else would you want to know?

____

____

____

____

____

Name: ______________________________ Date: ________________

Directions: Closely read these texts. Then, study the flyer on page 77. Look for words about soccer in each text. Write the words in the chart.

Close-Reading Texts

Kicking It with Beckham	Taking the Shot
Beckham grew up in England. He lived a simple life. He played soccer constantly as a young boy. He worked hard on his skills. It has always been the biggest part of his life. He played his first professional game in 1992 as a young man. He was only 17 years old. He played for the Manchester United team.	I was playing the forward position on that day and was running the ball up the field with my friend, Josie. We were passing it back and forth and making a lot of progress. We had practiced this all week. I could hear the crowd cheering and thought I even heard my mom yell my name. I was very focused, so all I could do was keep my eye on the ball and watch the goal.

Text	Nouns	Verbs
Kicking It with Beckham		
Taking the Shot		
Soccer Camp Flyer		

Name: ______________________ Date: ______________

Directions: Closely read these texts. Then, compare and contrast David Beckham with the narrator in the story.

Close-Reading Texts

Kicking It with Beckham	Taking the Shot
David Beckham got a lot of attention for one goal he made in 1996. During a game, he noticed a goalie who was out of the goal. He kicked a goal from the halfway line of the field. He made it! Many people started to notice Beckham after this play. He continued to work hard. Beckham helped his team win many games.	In an instant, I saw my chance. I could see a line straight through to the net. I was sure that the ball would sail right past the goalie. I planted my left foot and aimed my right leg toward the goal. I kicked that ball with all my might. I watched the ball go right into the goalie's hands. Then, I heard the whistle.

David Beckham	Narrator
Both	

Name: ______________________ Date: ____________

Directions: Think about the texts from this unit. Then, respond to the prompt.

You are the narrator in "Taking the Shot." You just went to your first day of soccer camp. Write a diary entry about your day. Describe what you did and how you felt. Draw a picture.

Name: ______________________ **Date:** ____________

Directions: Imagine David Beckham is going to be in your town. He is going to sign autographs. Design a flyer for the event. Make sure to give details about the event.

Name: ____________________ Date: ____________

Directions: Read the text, and answer the questions.

As You Read

Write at least one question or comment you have in the margins.

The First Chocolate Chip Cookie

Can you imagine a world with no chocolate chip cookies? This yummy treat did not always exist. It was invented by Ruth Wakefield. It happened in 1930. She worked at an inn. She baked treats for her guests. One night, she made a decision. She cut pieces off a chocolate bar. She added them to her cookie batter. She wanted to make a chocolate cookie. She thought it would melt together. She was surprised that the chocolate stayed in chunks!

1. Which question about the text would help readers check for understanding?
   - (A) What comes in chunks like chocolate?
   - (B) What else can people mix together?
   - (C) Who invented the chocolate chip cookie?
   - (D) Where is an inn near my house?

2. What alternative title reflects the main idea of the text?
   - (A) Mixing It Up
   - (B) A Delicious Surprise
   - (C) Types of Sweet Treats
   - (D) Treats for the Guests

3. Which word has the same vowel sound as *chip*?
   - (A) inn
   - (B) creek
   - (C) cheap
   - (D) type

4. What is the definition of *chunks* as it is used in this text?
   - (A) lumps
   - (B) rocks
   - (C) large pieces
   - (D) hard parts

Unit 5 WEEK 1 DAY 2

Name: ______________________ Date: ______________

Directions: Read the text, and answer the questions.

As You Read

Put a ? next to anything that is confusing, such as an unfamiliar word. Share your ? with a partner.

Food Tasters

Do you like to eat food? You could earn money doing that for a job! A food taster is a real career that many adults pursue. It is not as easy a job as you would think. Food tasters have to think a lot about how things smell, taste, and feel in their mouths. They have to be able to describe all of these sensations. Companies hire tasters to check their products before they go on store shelves.

1. What is the text mostly about?
   - Ⓐ what food tasters do
   - Ⓑ how much money food tasters make
   - Ⓒ types of food
   - Ⓓ the five senses

2. Which word is the root word in *tasters*?
   - Ⓐ toast
   - Ⓑ taster
   - Ⓒ taste
   - Ⓓ ster

3. Which word is a synonym for *pursue*?
   - Ⓐ hunt
   - Ⓑ go after
   - Ⓒ trail
   - Ⓓ look at

4. Which other type of text is most similar to this text?
   - Ⓐ a poem about the five senses
   - Ⓑ an article about unique jobs
   - Ⓒ a recipe in a cookbook
   - Ⓓ a journal entry of a taste tester

Name: ______________________ Date: ______________

Directions: Read the text, and answer the questions.

As You Read

Put a ! next to facts you find interesting. Share your ! with a partner.

Supertasters

Everyone prefers certain foods. We all have likes. We all have dislikes. Sometimes, our likes and dislikes change with age. Some people always taste food in a different way from other people. These people are supertasters. They have more taste buds. They have a very intense sense of taste. Supertasters are very sensitive to certain tastes. Bitter things taste even more bitter. Salty foods taste saltier. Sweet things may taste too sweet. Everything has more flavor, but that might not always be good.

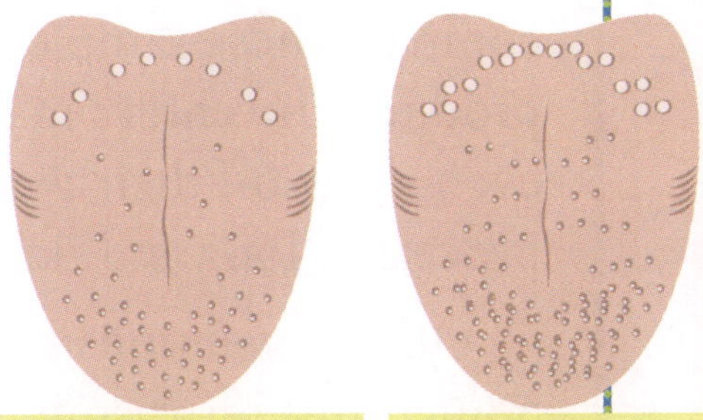

not a supertaster *supertaster*

1. What makes someone a supertaster?
   - (A) fewer taste buds
   - (B) a longer tongue
   - (C) more practice tasting foods
   - (D) more taste buds

2. Which word from the text makes a new word by adding the prefix *dis*–?
   - (A) sweet
   - (B) sure
   - (C) taste
   - (D) super

3. List at least three words the author uses to describe taste.

____

____

____

4. What do you think would be the pros and cons of being a supertaster?

____

____

____

Name: ______________________ Date: ____________

As You Read

Put a ! next to facts you find interesting. Put a ? next to anything that is confusing or that makes you wonder new things.

The Invention of Gum

Some inventors spend time trying to get an invention just right. They work hard on samples. They compare these samples. They try to get the very best product. Inventors may talk to other people. They may even show off their work to get ideas from others. The process is long and detailed.

Other inventions happen almost by accident. Something surprising might happen. This surprise then causes a person to have a new idea. That is all it takes. Chewing gum was invented this way. It came about by accident.

People have been chewing substances for many years. Early people chewed birch bark tar. And some people liked substances that came from plants or grasses.

What we call "chewing gum" was made by chance. People in Mexico liked to chew something called *chicle*. This was a sap from sapodilla trees. A general in the Mexican army wanted to use the chicle. He wanted to sell it as a cheaper alternative for rubber.

An American inventor became involved. His name was Thomas Adams. He could not get the chicle to work as a substitute for rubber. He used chicle to try to invent other things. One day, he popped the chicle into his mouth. He chewed it. He liked it. He added a flavor to the chicle. This was the first use of chewing gum.

Today, chewing gum is a very popular product in stores. It comes in many flavors. It comes in many sizes and shapes. Some chewing gum has sugar. Some does not. People chew gum for different reasons. One reason is to have good breath. Some people chew it to help them focus or to stop themselves from eating too many snacks. And some people just chew it because it tastes good.

Name: ______________________ Date: ____________

Directions: Read "The Invention of Gum." Then, answer the questions.

1. What is the purpose for reading this text?

- (A) to learn how to make gum
- (B) to be persuaded to buy gum
- (C) to learn about how gum was invented
- (D) to learn about all inventions

2. Who would likely make a strong connection to this text?

- (A) a teacher who is interested in different countries
- (B) a child who loves to see what happens in science experiments
- (C) an adult who speaks English and Spanish
- (D) an adult who was a general in the war

3. What point does the author make in this text?

- (A) Inventions happen in all sorts of ways.
- (B) Inventions take a lot of time.
- (C) Inventions require a lot of hard work.
- (D) Inventors are usually lucky.

4. How does this text describe the invention of gum?

- (A) It was a longtime experiment.
- (B) It was a scientific breakthrough.
- (C) It was a happy accident.
- (D) It was a mistake.

5. Write three things that led to the chewing gum we know today.

1.	
2.	
3.	

Name: ______________________ Date: ______________

Directions: Reread "The Invention of Gum." Then, respond to the prompt.

Write your own fictional story about chewing gum. Describe a sequence of events that led to its invention. Use your imagination. Draw an illustration to support your story.

Name: ______________________________ Date: ______________

Directions: Read the text, and answer the questions.

As You Read

Underline words or phrases that describe the character's actions.

Sharing Sweets

Sukun started the school year with a huge smile. He had spent the summer with his family in Cambodia. Sukun's aunt taught him lots of dessert recipes. Now, he wanted to share them with his friends. When the bell rang for lunch, Sukun leapt to his feet and raced to the door. He had a skip in his step on the way to the cafeteria.

1. Why is Sukun excited for lunch at school?
   - (A) He wants to try the new cafeteria food.
   - (B) He wants to trade lunches with his friend.
   - (C) He wants to share a dessert he made with friends.
   - (D) He wants to introduce his aunt to his friends.

2. Who is the main character?
   - (A) Sukun's aunt
   - (B) Sukun
   - (C) Sukun's friend
   - (D) Sukun's brother

3. Where did Sukun spend his summer?
   - (A) in summer school
   - (B) in Cambodia
   - (C) in Canada
   - (D) at his friend's house

4. What is the past tense of *leap*?
   - (A) leapt
   - (B) leaped
   - (C) loped
   - (D) leak

Name: ______________________________ Date: ______________

Directions: Read the text, and answer the questions.

As You Read

Write at least one question or thought you have about the text in the margins.

Nom Lort at Lunch

"I made you some nom lort," Sukun said to his friends. "It's a Cambodian dessert made of jelly in coconut sauce."

"What does the jelly taste like?" asked Alana.

"It's pandan flavored," Sukun explained.

"Panda?" Alana yelped.

Sukun chuckled and said, "Pan-*dan* leaves are sweet, and they taste sort of like grass."

Alana considered the dish for a minute, then shook her head. "Sorry, Sukun. I don't want to eat grass."

Cory nodded. "I'm with Alana. Pandan sounds cool, but this looks clumpy and slimy. It's too much for me."

Sukun put the lid back on his container of nom lort. His smile faded, his shoulders slumped, and he hung his head.

1. What is nom lort?

- (A) a dessert
- (B) an appetizer
- (C) a soup
- (D) a salad

2. What does Sukun say pandan tastes like?

- (A) sweet and grass-like
- (B) sour coconut
- (C) cold oatmeal
- (D) salty cheese

3. What can readers infer from the sentence, *His smile faded, his shoulders slumped, and he hung his head*?

- (A) Sukun is nervous to try the nom lort in his lunch.
- (B) Sukun is sad his friends don't want to try his food.
- (C) Sukun is happy he gets to eat all of his nom lort.
- (D) Sukun is full.

4. Which word is used as an adjective in the text?

- (A) sauce
- (B) leaves
- (C) chuckled
- (D) clumpy

Name: ______________________ Date: ______________

Directions: Read the text, and answer the questions.

As You Read

Write a ∞ wherever you make connections. Write a few words in the margins to describe the connection.

The Baking Contest

Sukun spent the rest of the day pondering what his friends had said. *Why are they so afraid to try something new?* he thought to himself. *A lot of the stuff they eat looks just as weird.*

Just then, his teacher, Ms. Bellows, handed him a flier.

"Class, may I have your attention?" Ms. Bellows asked. "To celebrate the holidays, there will be a baking contest in the cafeteria this Friday. Please fill out this form to sign up."

Sukun began to smile. He had a spectacular idea.

1. What is a synonym for *great*?

- (A) cafeteria
- (B) spectacular
- (C) celebrate
- (D) new

2. Why does Sukun begin to smile?

- (A) He tasted a new dessert.
- (B) His teacher told a joke.
- (C) He got a good idea.
- (D) His friends liked his food.

3. How is the school celebrating the holidays?

____

4. Write a prediction about what you think will happen next in the story.

____

____

Name: ______________________________ Date: ______________

As You Read

Write a ∞ wherever you make connections.

New Flavors for Old Friends

Sukun stayed busy the night before the baking contest. He mixed up a batch of sponge cake batter. He flavored it with pandan extract and colored it bright green. Next, he whipped butter and sugar into a fluffy frosting. He flavored it with coconut milk and slathered it on his cake.

"Now, I'll decorate it with Cambodian desserts," Sukun said.

He picked out each teardrop-shaped piece of jelly from his nom lort. He arranged the lort into flower shapes on top of the cake. Then, he used the same ingredients to make *cendol*. This kind of jelly came in long strands, like noodles. Sukun draped them across his cake like vines. Finally, he made mung bean dumplings. Sukun mashed mung beans and sugar into a paste. He made a dough from rice flour. He rolled the bean paste into balls and covered them with dough.

"All I have to do is boil these dumplings," said Sukun. "Then, I'll drizzle the whole cake with coconut milk syrup!"

Sukun's cake turned out perfect. It looked like a garden full of leaves, flowers, and rocks. The next day at school, no one was surprised when Sukun won the baking contest. But he didn't really care what the judges thought. As soon as he got his ribbon, Sukun dashed to his cake. He served up two slices and rushed to his friends.

"Cory! Alana! I want you to try this," Sukun said. "I thought you'd like Cambodian dessert more this way."

"Sukun, that looks amazing!" Alana couldn't contain her excitement.

"Yeah, dude, I can't wait to try it," Cory agreed.

Alana slurped a bit of cendol off her fork. Cory plucked a mung bean dumpling off his slice.

"This jelly has a neat texture! It's like sweet spaghetti," said Alana.

"This dumpling is great," Cory said. "I never thought I'd like beans in dessert!"

"Pandan tastes interesting," Alana said. "Sorry I didn't try it earlier."

"I'm sorry, too. Cambodian food is great. Thanks for sharing," said Cory.

Sukun grinned and threw his arms around his friends. "I'm always happy to share. I forgive you, but only if you both make me a cake this weekend!"

135045—180 Days of Reading

Name: ______________________ Date: ______________

Directions: Read "New Flavors for Old Friends." Then, answer the questions.

1. Where is one setting in this part of the story?

- (A) the school cafeteria
- (B) Cambodia
- (C) Sukun's backyard
- (D) a restaurant

2. What does Alana compare cendol to?

- (A) nom lort
- (B) a garden
- (C) sweet spaghetti
- (D) vines

3. Which statement is true about Sukun?

- (A) He wants his friends to like his dessert.
- (B) He does not like to cook or bake.
- (C) He does not care what his friends think.
- (D) He worries about what the judges think.

4. What message can readers learn from this story?

- (A) If food looks different, it probably tastes bad.
- (B) It is important to win every contest.
- (C) Don't be afraid to try new and different things.
- (D) Always do your best in school.

5. Write details about the story elements of the text.

Characters	**Setting**
Sukun's Problem	**Solution**

Name: ______________________ Date: ______________

Directions: Reread "New Flavors for Old Friends." Then, respond to the prompt.

Write a book review for this story. Share your opinion of the story. Would you recommend it to someone else? Why or why not?

Name: ______________________ Date: ______________

Script for Carnadent TV Commercial

Carnadent, the clean-teeth beef!

Time to toss that old toothbrush. Say goodbye to toothpaste. This ground beef product is full of germ-killing chemicals.

Carnadent is easy to use. First, cook up a patty to activate its power. Then, chew for cleaner teeth. Finally, swallow for fresher breath.

Now, go show off that dazzling smile!

Try Carnadent today!

(say the following very quickly)

This product is not recommended by most dentists. It is made with 60% beef. We do not know what the other 40% is. The use of these chemicals in food has not been approved by law. So far, no customers have reported more dazzling smiles after use.

Name: ______________________ Date: ______________

Directions: Read "Script for Carnadent TV Commercial." Then, answer the questions.

1. What does the commercial tell people to do first when using Carnadent?

- (A) chew it
- (B) cook up a patty
- (C) swallow it
- (D) brush their teeth

2. What is the purpose of this text?

- (A) to entertain readers with a silly ad
- (B) to inform readers how to care for their teeth
- (C) to describe a new toothpaste
- (D) to entertain readers with a story

3. Which word has the same root word as *recommended*?

- (A) recommendation
- (B) mending
- (C) comedy
- (D) celebration

4. Which word is a compound word?

- (A) chemicals
- (B) dazzling
- (C) customers
- (D) toothpaste

5. Write clues from the text that let you know it is a fictional, or fake, commercial.

Clues

Name: ______________________________ Date: ______________

Directions: Closely read these texts. Then, compare and contrast Ruth Wakefield with the character Sukun.

Close-Reading Texts

The First Chocolate Chip Cookie	New Flavors for Old Friends
Can you imagine a world with no chocolate chip cookies? This yummy treat did not always exist. It was invented by Ruth Wakefield. It happened in 1930. She worked at an inn. She baked treats for her guests. One night, she made a decision. She cut pieces off a chocolate bar. She added them to her cookie batter. She wanted to make a chocolate cookie. She thought it would melt together. She was surprised that the chocolate stayed in chunks!	Sukun stayed busy the night before the baking contest. He mixed up a batch of sponge cake batter. He flavored it with pandan extract and colored it bright green. Next, he whipped butter and sugar into a fluffy frosting. He flavored it with coconut milk and slathered it on his cake. "Now, I'll decorate it with Cambodian desserts," Sukun said.

Ruth Wakefield	Sukun

Both

Name: ______________________ Date: ______________

Directions: Closely read these texts. Study the TV commercial on page 95. Then, write about the author's purpose for each of these texts. There can be more than one purpose for each text.

Close-Reading Texts

The Invention of Gum	New Flavors for Old Friends
People in Mexico liked to chew something called *chicle*. This was a sap from sapodilla trees. A general in the Mexican army wanted to use the chicle. He wanted to sell it as a cheaper alternative for rubber. An American inventor became involved. His name was Thomas Adams. He could not get the chicle to work as a substitute for rubber. He used chicle to try to invent other things. One day, he popped the chicle into his mouth. He chewed it. He liked it. He added a flavor to the chicle.	He picked out each teardrop-shaped piece of jelly from his nom lort. He arranged the lort into flower shapes on top of the cake. Then, he used the same ingredients to make *cendol*. This kind of jelly came in long strands, like noodles. Sukun draped them across his cake like vines. Finally, he made mung bean dumplings. Sukun mashed mung beans and sugar into a paste. He made a dough from rice flour. He rolled the bean paste into balls and covered them with dough.

Author's Purpose		
The Invention of Gum	**New Flavors for Old Friends**	**Script for Carnadent TV Commercial**

Name: ______________________________ Date: ______________

Directions: Think about the texts from this unit. Then, respond to the prompt.

Write a detailed description of your favorite food or meal. Describe it with all of your senses.

____

____

____

____

____

____

____

____

____

____

____

____

____

Name: ______________________________ Date: ______________

Directions: Think of your own fictional, or fake, product. Will it help you study for tests? Or maybe it is a new hair product. Write a script for a TV advertisement for your product. Draw a picture of your product.

____

____

____

____

____

____

____

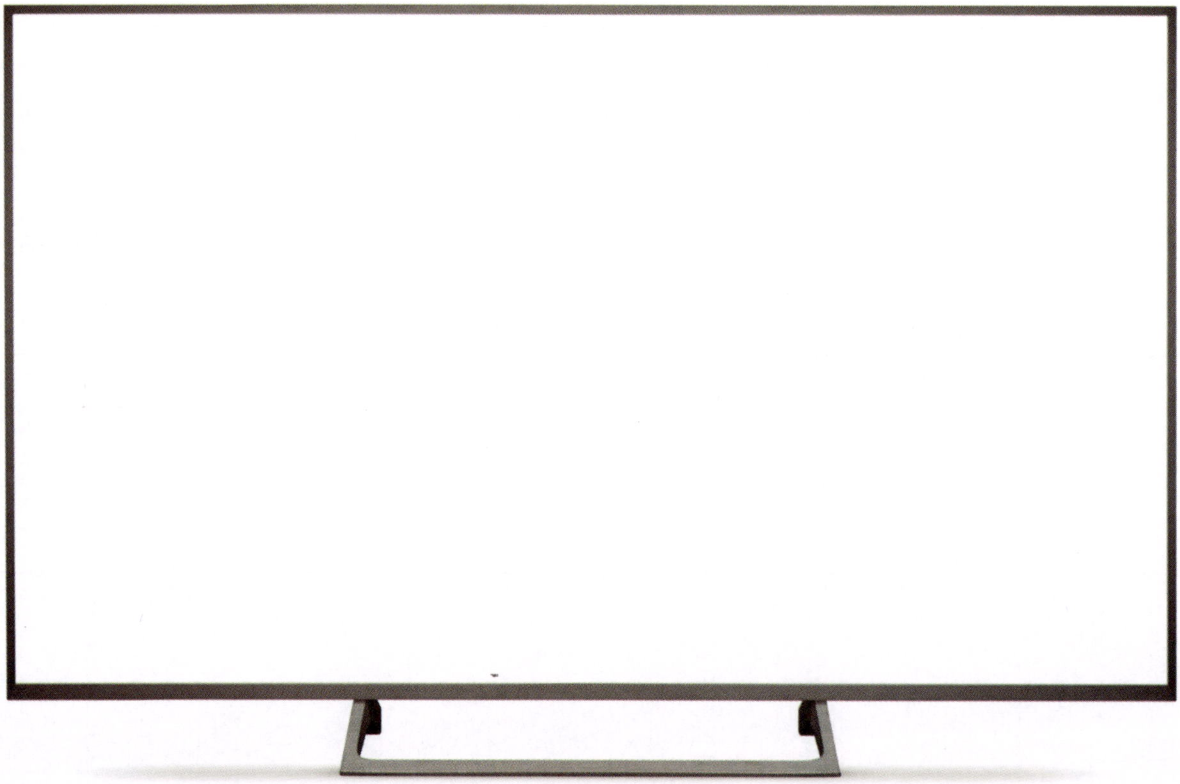

Name: ______________________ Date: ______________

Directions: Read the text, and answer the questions.

As You Read

Underline details that describe how Earth moves.

Earth's Movement

Earth is always moving. Earth revolves around the sun once each year. This creates the four different seasons. Earth also rotates around its axis every 24 hours. This is what causes night and day. The night sky changes throughout the year. Our view of the constellations changes with each season.

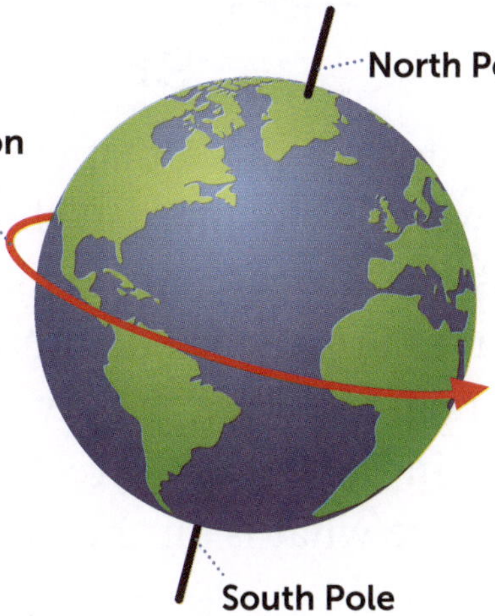

1. What is the main idea?

- (A) Earth rotates around the sun in 24 hours.
- (B) Earth revolves around the sun in one year.
- (C) Earth revolves and rotates.
- (D) The night sky changes.

2. Which two words have the same vowel sound?

- (A) *year* and *with*
- (B) *sky* and *night*
- (C) *in* and *night*
- (D) *our* and *for*

3. Which object would rotate?

- (A) a book
- (B) a snake
- (C) a wheel
- (D) a kite

4. The language of the text suggests that the author is addressing ________.

- (A) Earth
- (B) the author
- (C) all humans
- (D) the sun

Name: ______________________________ Date: ______________

Directions: Read the text, and answer the questions.

As You Read

Underline facts that are new to you. Put stars next to any facts you already know.

Star Charts

A star chart is a map of the night sky. It is also known as a sky map. It shows where stars and constellations are located in the sky. Like most maps, a star chart is labeled with the four directions. When a person observes the sky, it helps to hold the star chart in the correct direction. Then it is easy to compare what is on the map with what is in the sky.

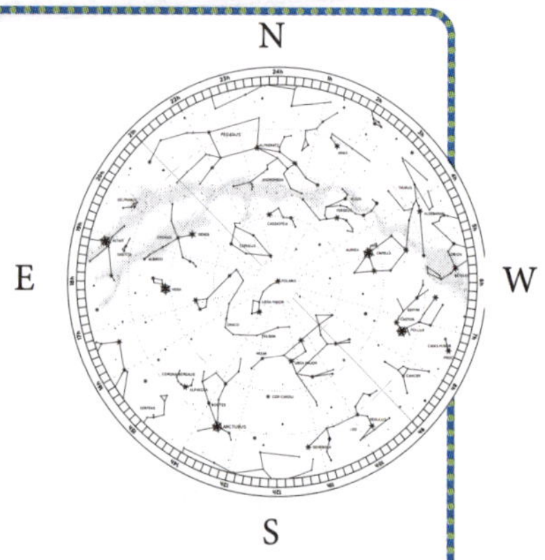

1. Which best summarizes the main idea?
   - (A) Constellations tell stories.
   - (B) The night sky is dark.
   - (C) Star charts are maps of the night sky.
   - (D) Map words are important.

2. Which words have the same vowel sound?
   - (A) *like* and *is*
   - (B) *use* and *four*
   - (C) *star* and *chart*
   - (D) *sky* and *point*

3. Why might someone use a star chart?
   - (A) to find a constellation in the sky
   - (B) to know directions
   - (C) to tell what time of day it is
   - (D) to find a star's distance from Earth

4. How are star charts and sky maps related?
   - (A) They are two different names for the same item.
   - (B) They must be used together to watch the sky.
   - (C) A star chart used to be called a sky map.
   - (D) A start chart is used to create a sky map.

Name: ______________________________ Date: ______________

Directions: Read the text, and answer the questions.

As You Read

Circle words that identify objects in space.

Astronomy

Astronomy is a type of science. It looks at the universe. The universe is made up of many things. People who study the universe are called *astronomers*. They use special tools to learn about space. They look at objects in space. And they can even listen to space. Astronomers often pick one thing to investigate. They may focus on planets. They may study stars or the sun. They may learn about black holes. This information is helpful. People around the world use it to learn about space.

1. Which word does **not** mean the same as *investigate*?
   - (A) study
   - (B) explore
   - (C) examine
   - (D) ignore

2. What other type of text is similar to this text?
   - (A) a science book
   - (B) a fantasy novel
   - (C) a picture of the planet Mars
   - (D) a journal entry about a trip to a history museum

3. What is the main idea of this text?

____

4. If you could add another photo to the text on this page, what would it be? How could it help readers learn more?

____

____

Name: ______________________ Date: ______________

As You Read

Write questions or thoughts you have about the text in the margins. Underline the parts of the text you comment on.

The Night Sky

People say that the sky is dark at night. But there are a lot of stars in the night sky. These stars twinkle and provide a lot of light. There is a lot to look at in the night sky! The stars in the sky have guided people for centuries. Humans have always looked up to the sky. People have used the stars as a way to show direction.

Over time, stories have been told about the star patterns. These patterns are called *constellations*. There are 88 official constellations. They divide the night sky. They change position slightly each season.

Many constellations are named from old Greek myths. The Greeks were one of the first cultures to create names for stars. They believed the star patterns were made by the gods. They named these patterns after animals and objects. They also named 12 patterns that make up the signs of the zodiac.

One star that is often used as a guide is called *Polaris*. Some stargazers say it is the brightest star in the sky. Polaris is also known as the North Star. It never rises or sets. It stays put in the sky. People can easily find Polaris. They notice that it belongs to a well-known constellation. Polaris is at the end of the handle of the Little Dipper. The Big Dipper and the Little Dipper are constellations that are easy to find.

One way stargazers try to preserve the night sky is by fighting light pollution. This is not a type of pollution that most people consider. But it is very important to people who like to look at stars. Light pollution occurs when too many lights are on in an area. The lights may be from homes or cars. Businesses use a lot of light, too. Light makes it hard for people to see patterns in the dark sky.

Name: ______________________ Date: ______________

Directions: Read "The Night Sky." Then, answer the questions.

1. Which description of this text is the most accurate?
   - (A) This is about someone hoping for a falling star.
   - (B) This is about finding constellations in the night sky.
   - (C) This is about living away from the city where you can see the stars clearly.
   - (D) This is about how the Big Dipper got its name.

2. What is the author's purpose?
   - (A) to describe each constellation
   - (B) to inform readers about the night sky
   - (C) to share Greek mythology
   - (D) to compare the night sky and the day sky

3. Which statement shows a strong personal connection to the text?
   - (A) The Big Dipper is the name of my favorite restaurant.
   - (B) I have read some myths before.
   - (C) I have used a star chart to look at constellations.
   - (D) I don't like darkness.

4. Why is light pollution a problem?
   - (A) Light pollution happens when lights shine on air pollution.
   - (B) It must be pitch black to see any stars.
   - (C) It is hard to see constellations when there are too many lights.
   - (D) People who watch stars often leave garbage on the ground.

5. Write the main topic or idea of each paragraph.

Paragraph 1	
Paragraph 2	
Paragraph 3	
Paragraph 4	
Paragraph 5	

Name: ______________________________ Date: ______________

Directions: Reread "The Night Sky." Then, respond to the prompt.

Think about what you know about the night sky or have seen yourself. What personal connections can you make with this text? What connections can you make to the world or to other texts you have read? Write about them using complete sentences.

____

____

____

____

____

____

____

____

____

____

____

____

____

Name: ______________________ Date: ____________

Directions: Read the text, and answer the questions.

As You Read

Underline words or phrases that describe the characters.

Loris and Her Diamond Spoon

There was once a friendly old woman named Loris who lived in a tiny hut in a faraway kingdom. She stirred her soup with a diamond spoon. All the people thought her soup was the best in the land. They thought her talent shone as bright as her diamond spoon. Loris's soup was so splendid that even the Queen was jealous of it.

"My chefs can make a soup twice as good as hers," said the Queen. But her chefs could concoct no such soup, and she knew it.

1. Which word describes the Queen?

- (A) friendly
- (B) jealous
- (C) tiny
- (D) bright

2. What does Loris use to stir her soup?

- (A) a wooden stick
- (B) a fancy blender
- (C) a diamond spoon
- (D) a magic wand

3. Which is an example of a prepositional phrase?

- (A) in a faraway kingdom
- (B) so splendid
- (C) and she knew it
- (D) friendly old woman

4. What is the definition of *concoct*?

- (A) to taste
- (B) a feeling of excitement
- (C) to make or create
- (D) to cook slowly

Name: ______________________________ Date: ______________

Directions: Read the text, and answer the questions.

As You Read

Put a ? next to anything that is confusing or that makes you wonder about something.

Diamond Heist

So, the Queen hatched a devious plan.

"I'll order my knights to sneak into Loris's home. Then, I'll steal her diamond spoon. Her soup will taste disgusting! Then, everyone must come to my palace to have the best soup in the country," cackled the Queen.

That night, the Queen's knights snuck into Loris's tiny hut. They came out with a diamond spoon. The Queen's chefs used the spoon to stir up a fresh pot of soup. The Queen was almost drooling when she brought the diamond spoon to her lips.

"Pah! It tastes the same as before," she spat, and she threw the spoon into the sky. The diamond spoon got stuck among the stars.

1. Why does the Queen want to steal the diamond spoon?

- (A) She wants to give it as a gift to her chefs.
- (B) She wants to have the prettiest spoon.
- (C) She thinks it will make her soup taste the best.
- (D) She thinks it will make her soup healthier.

2. Which words are homophones?

- (A) *spoon* and *spun*
- (B) *nights* and *knights*
- (C) *palace* and *place*
- (D) *steal* and *still*

3. What does the Queen do after she tastes the soup?

- (A) She takes a sip of water.
- (B) She bangs the spoon on the table.
- (C) She throws the spoon into the sky.
- (D) She thanks the chefs for making the soup.

4. Which word best describes the Queen's actions at the beginning of this text?

- (A) sneaky
- (B) strange
- (C) thoughtful
- (D) helpful

Name: ______________________ Date: ______________

Directions: Read the text, and answer the questions.

As You Read

Put a ! next to events you find surprising or interesting.

A Second Spoon

The next day, Loris still woke up her village with a pot of her very best soup. The Queen was furious. She stormed into Loris's village. She slammed her scepter into the ground, right next to Loris's hut.

"Come out, you filthy old woman," screeched the Queen.

"Good morning, your majesty," said Loris. "Would you like a bowl of my very best soup?"

The Queen's mouth nearly hit the ground. Loris was holding a diamond spoon that was twice as large as the other.

"Oh, this old thing? It's awfully heavy, but I can't seem to find my little spoon," said Loris.

The Queen huffed and puffed and snatched the diamond spoon right out of Loris's hand.

1. What happens last?
   - (A) Loris wakes up.
   - (B) The Queen tries some soup.
   - (C) The Queen grabs the diamond spoon.
   - (D) The Queen goes to Loris's hut.

2. What is the definition of *stormed* as it is used in this text?
   - (A) rained heavily
   - (B) walked or stomped angrily
   - (C) grabbed quickly
   - (D) moved or walked slowly

3. Write two action words or phrases that show the Queen is upset.

   ____

   ____

4. What are some things you do that show how you are feeling?

   ____

   ____

   ____

Name: ______________________________ Date: ______________

As You Read

Put a ! next to events you find surprising or interesting.

Skyful of Diamonds

"This giant diamond spoon must be her secret," said the Queen. She brought it back to her palace and gave it to her chefs. Her chefs stirred up yet another pot of soup. They gathered the most flavorful spices. They chopped the freshest vegetables. They roasted the juiciest cuts of meat. The chefs stirred, simmered, and seasoned the soup for hours on end. Finally, they served it to the Queen in a golden bowl with rose petals on top. But yet again, the Queen said, "Pah! It tastes exactly the same!" This time, she had to use both arms to throw the diamond spoon. Up into the sky it went, and it got stuck among the stars as well.

Meanwhile, Loris was still stirring her very best soup. She had found a big stick outside. She washed the stick in the river. Then, she dragged her big pot out of her hut. Loris invited all the people in the village to come have some soup. "Everyone, please bring your own spoons today," Loris said to the crowd.

Just then, the Queen came speeding into the village. Her face was sweaty, and her crown was tilted to one side. She was so angry! She had run all the way from the palace.

"You lying, lowdown snake," hissed the Queen. "Your diamond spoons are no good at all! What's the *real* secret to your delicious soup? You'd better tell me this instant."

Loris shrugged and said, "There's no secret, my Queen. My diamond spoons were just gifts from travelers who enjoyed my soup. I offer soup to anyone in need of a warm meal. Would you like the recipe?"

The Queen's mouth hung open. She hadn't realized she could have simply *asked* for the soup recipe. The Queen was so embarrassed that she shuffled all the way back to her palace. She was too proud to take the recipe. She never spoke to Loris again. Each night after that, the Queen hated looking at the sky. She was haunted by the two twinkling diamond spoons. People in the kingdom called them the *Big Dipper* and the *Little Dipper*. But only the Queen knew her shameful truth. She had been cruel to a talented cook, and in return, Loris had been kind. And so, the Queen spent the rest of her life trying and failing to pull those diamond spoons out of the stars.

Name: ______________________ Date: ____________

Directions: Read "Skyful of Diamonds." Then, answer the questions.

1. What is one setting in the story?

- (A) the village square
- (B) the Queen's bedroom
- (C) Loris's hut
- (D) the dungeon

2. Which word best describes how the queen feels at the end of the story?

- (A) regretful
- (B) confused
- (C) happy
- (D) scared

3. What happens first?

- (A) The Queen runs to the village.
- (B) The Queen throws the spoon in the sky.
- (C) The Queen gives the spoon to her chefs.
- (D) The Queen asks Loris for her secret.

4. Which adjective best describes Loris's actions in the text?

- (A) unusual
- (B) secretive
- (C) generous
- (D) mean

5. Describe the beginning, middle, and end of the story.

Beginning	Middle	End

Name: ______________________________ **Date:** ______________

Directions: Reread "Skyful of Diamonds." Then, respond to the prompt.

Write your own version of how the story ends. Add to or change it to make it different.

"Would you like the recipe?"

Name: ______________________ Date: ______________

ASTROVIEW PLANETARIUM

Schedule

Witness the stars above at

Tonight's Sky.

Playing at 10:00 a.m. daily.

Learn about the latest technology at

Space Robots Advance.

Playing at 3:00 p.m. daily.

Spot footage from another world at

Aliens...or Not???

Playing at 7:00 p.m. daily.

Prices

Adults … $20

Children (age 12 and under) … $6

Students (with valid student ID card) … $12

Seniors (age 65 and over) … $8

The 1st Sunday of every month is free.

The 3rd Thursday of every month is Senior Date Night. Dance under the stars from 3:00 to 7:00 p.m. ($20, must be age 65 and over.)

Name: ______________________________ Date: ______________

Directions: Read "Astroview Planetarium." Then, answer the questions.

1. What plays at 3:00 p.m. daily?

- Ⓐ *Aliens… or Not???*
- Ⓑ *Space Robots Advance*
- Ⓒ *Tonight's Sky*
- Ⓓ *The Great Unknown*

2. Who would be charged $8 for a ticket?

- Ⓐ a child who is 10 years old
- Ⓑ a person who is 68 years old
- Ⓒ a person who is 42 years old
- Ⓓ a student

3. People can visit planetariums to learn about ______.

- Ⓐ famous people
- Ⓑ animals
- Ⓒ the ocean
- Ⓓ space

4. Which word has three syllables?

- Ⓐ technology
- Ⓑ aliens
- Ⓒ robots
- Ⓓ footage

5. Which show at the Astroview Planetarium would you most like to attend? Why?

____

____

____

____

____

____

____

____

Name: ______________________ Date: ______________

Directions: Closely read this text. Study "Astroview Planetarium" on page 113. Look for words or phrases about space in each text. Write them in the chart. Use three of the words or phrases to write your own sentences.

Close-Reading Texts

Astronomy
Astronomy is a type of science. It looks at the universe. The universe is made up of many things. People who study the universe are called *astronomers*. They use special tools to learn about space. They look at objects in space. And they can even listen to space. Astronomers often pick one thing to investigate. They may focus on planets. They may study stars or the sun. They may learn about black holes. This information is helpful. People around the world use it to learn about space.

Text	Space Words
Astronomy	
Astroview Planetarium	

1. ______________________

2. ______________________

3. ______________________

Name: ______________________ Date: ____________

Directions: Closely read these texts. Then, compare and contrast the two texts. Think about their purposes, tones, language, genres, and structures.

Close-Reading Texts

The Night Sky	One star that is often used as a guide is called *Polaris.* Some stargazers say it is the brightest star in the sky. Polaris is also known as the North Star. It never rises or sets. It stays put in the sky. People can easily find Polaris. They notice that it belongs to a well-known constellation. Polaris is at the end of the handle of the Little Dipper. The Big Dipper and the Little Dipper are constellations that are easy to find.
A Skyful of Diamonds	The Queen was so embarrassed that she shuffled all the way back to her palace. She was too proud to take the recipe. She never spoke to Loris again. Each night after that, the Queen hated looking at the sky. She was haunted by the two twinkling diamond spoons. People in the kingdom called them the *Big Dipper* and the *Little Dipper*. But only the Queen knew her shameful truth. She had been cruel to a talented cook, and in return, Loris had been kind. And so, the Queen spent the rest of her life trying and failing to pull those diamond spoons out of the stars.

The Night Sky

Both

A Skyful of Diamonds

Name: ______________________________ Date: ______________

Directions: Think about the texts from this unit. Then, respond to the prompt.

Choose a constellation in the sky. Write your own story about how it came to be. Draw a picture to go with your story.

Name: ______________________ Date: ______________

Directions: You run a small zoo in your town. You need to create a poster to put at the front. It should give prices and a schedule of events. It can have other information you think is important. Design your poster in the space below.

Name: ______________________ Date: ______________

Directions: Read the text, and answer the questions.

As You Read

Underline facts about insects. Put stars by the ones you find most interesting.

Insects

Insects can be very different. Some insects fly. Some insects only walk, run, or jump. Some insects help people, and others harm people. But insects have some things in common. Insects are invertebrates, which means they have no backbone. All insects have the same three body parts: a head, an abdomen, and a thorax. All insects have three pairs of legs and two pairs of wings.

1. Which question about the text would help readers monitor their reading?

- (A) Who has an abdomen?
- (B) How are insects different?
- (C) What would I do if I had wings?
- (D) Who has broken a bone?

2. What suffix could you add to the root word *help* to make a new word?

- (A) *–er*
- (B) *–ly*
- (C) *–est*
- (D) *–ion*

3. What is an antonym for *harm*?

- (A) hate
- (B) hit
- (C) help
- (D) bite

4. Which word describes the tone of this text?

- (A) factual
- (B) angry
- (C) funny
- (D) persuasive

Name: ______________________________ Date: ______________

Directions: Read the text, and answer the questions.

As You Read

Circle words or phrases that describe what monarch butterflies eat or drink.

Monarch Butterflies

Monarch butterflies eat plants. This makes them herbivores. Caterpillars only eat milkweed leaves. Adult monarchs like to drink nectar. They find nectar in milkweed. They also find it in other wildflowers. Certain garden flowers attract monarchs, too. People put these plants in their gardens. They hope the plants will draw monarchs in. They want to see them fly through!

1. What does the first sentence say about this text?
   - (A) It is about how monarchs migrate.
   - (B) It is about how monarchs navigate.
   - (C) It is about what monarchs eat.
   - (D) It is about plants that monarchs live in.

2. Which index entry would help a reader find this information?
   - (A) milkweed leaves
   - (B) nectar
   - (C) diet of monarchs
   - (D) all of the above

3. Which word has the same root word as *plants*?
   - (A) pants
   - (B) planting
   - (C) ant
   - (D) ants

4. What does *attract* mean in this text?
   - (A) see clearly
   - (B) hear clearly
   - (C) bring in
   - (D) match closely

Name: ______________________________ Date: ______________

Directions: Read the text, and answer the questions.

As You Read

Put a ? next to things that make you wonder about new things. Write your questions in the margins.

Names for Monarch Butterflies

William of Orange

Monarch butterflies have different names. The word *monarch* means "king" or "queen." Monarch butterflies get their name from a king. They used to have the nickname King Billy. This was a nickname for the king of England. He used to be the prince of Orange. This referred to a region in France, not the color. But monarch butterflies are orange and black, so the name stuck! Today, monarchs are also known as milkweed butterflies. Some people even call them *wanderers*. This is because they travel long distances.

1. Which question would help readers monitor their reading?
   - (A) What were all the kings and queens of England?
   - (B) Who is a wanderer?
   - (C) What are different names for monarch butterflies?
   - (D) Where is England?

2. Which of these is another name for monarch butterflies?
   - (A) travelers
   - (B) emperors
   - (C) milkweeds
   - (D) King Billys

3. Summarize how the monarch butterfly got its name.

   ____

   ____

4. Why do you think the author wrote this text?

   ____

Name: ______________________ Date: ______________

As You Read

Underline words or phrases that tell you about how butterflies survive.

The Delicate Lives of Monarch Butterflies

monarch butterfly

Monarch butterflies are stunning. Their colors and patterns are beautiful. They are easy to spot as they fly through the air. Monarchs start life as eggs. Then, they hatch as caterpillars. This phase lasts for about two weeks. Then, each caterpillar creates a chrysalis (KRIS-uh-lis), or a hard shell. Changes take place inside. Soon, a butterfly emerges!

The bright colors of monarchs are quite striking. Some people think the colors would attract predators. But they actually protect the butterfly from predators. This is called an *adaptation*. This is a feature an animal develops. It helps them increase their odds of survival. This change begins when monarchs are caterpillars. Caterpillars eat milkweed leaves. These leaves have a poisonous chemical. The caterpillars store the chemical in their bodies. It does not harm them. It makes them taste horrible to predators. Predators do not want to eat them.

Monarchs migrate from a summer to a winter habitat. They may be the only butterfly species to do this. Most start their migration in September or October. They travel the same routes each year. Their journey is divided by many stops. Each night, monarchs stop to rest or feed. They gather in a tree. This may be a eucalyptus tree. It could be a pine or a cypress. A single tree can have thousands of monarchs in it. This trip can take up to 90 days.

This migration faces problems, though. The main problem occurs when people cut down trees. The trees are logged. People use the wood for building. They want the open space, too. They want to build on the land. So, the monarchs can no longer take shelter in the trees. They cannot stop to rest. They cannot stay warm.

Some people are trying to help monarchs. They are protecting their habitats. People are planting milkweed. They are planting other flowers, too. People want monarchs to have food and water. They also want them to have shelter. These things will keep this beautiful species alive.

Name: ______________________ Date: ______________

Directions: Read "The Delicate Lives of Monarch Butterflies." Then, answer the questions.

1. How does the author feel about butterfly habitats being destroyed?

Ⓐ It is a serious problem.

Ⓑ It is okay because more trees will grow.

Ⓒ It should not matter because buildings are important.

Ⓓ It is funny because the butterflies are so silly.

2. Which topic is **not** covered in this text?

Ⓐ how and where monarchs migrate

Ⓑ how monarchs use their colors as an adaptation

Ⓒ how monarchs care for their young

Ⓓ what is happening to the monarch habitat

3. Which is the main idea of the text?

Ⓐ Monarch butterflies start their migration in the fall and travel for months.

Ⓑ Monarch butterflies are amazing creatures whose habitats are in danger.

Ⓒ Milkweed leaves are important but have a poisonous chemical.

Ⓓ Monarch butterflies start life as an egg.

4. Why are butterfly habitats in danger?

Ⓐ Wildfires are breaking out.

Ⓑ Air pollution has killed the butterflies.

Ⓒ Trees are being cut down.

Ⓓ Predators now live in their habitats.

5. Write a detail about each topic related to monarch butterflies listed in the chart.

Topic	Details
caterpillars	
chrysalis	
migration	
habitat	

Name: ______________________________ Date: ______________

Directions: Reread "The Delicate Lives of Monarch Butterflies." Then, respond to the prompt.

Think about what you know about monarch butterflies. Think about how monarch butterflies' habitats are in danger. What are some things you could do to help them? Describe your ideas in complete sentences.

____

____

____

____

____

____

____

____

____

____

____

____

Name: ______________________ Date: ______________

Directions: Read the text, and answer the questions.

As You Read

Underline words or phrases that tell how the character is feeling.

Butterflies in My Stomach

The morning bell rings loud in my ears, and my armpits start sweating. Today, the class is going to present our science projects. We've been working on them for the last two weeks. I made a huge poster about the Cairns birdwing butterfly. I wish I'd chosen a different subject, though. I feel like my stomach is full of butterflies right now. I look around the classroom and notice everyone else's posters. Most kids' handwriting is neater than mine. Their drawings are better, too. My cheeks feel hot.

At the front of the room, Mr. Lopez reaches into a cup full of straws to choose who will go first. My hands are shaking. His fingers close around a straw, and…

"Justin, please present your project," he says.

My eyes go wide, and I freeze.

1. What is one way readers know the narrator is nervous?

- (A) He chooses the Cairns birdwing butterfly.
- (B) He makes a huge poster.
- (C) His cheeks are hot.
- (D) He looks at other posters.

2. What is the setting?

- (A) a theater
- (B) a classroom
- (C) a garden
- (D) a playground

3. How many syllables are in the word *handwriting*?

- (A) one syllable
- (B) two syllables
- (C) three syllables
- (D) four syllables

4. What is the narrator's name?

- (A) Justin
- (B) Mr. Lopez
- (C) Cairns
- (D) Jason

Name: ______________________________ Date: ______________

Directions: Read the text, and answer the questions.

As You Read

Underline words or phrases that tell how the character is feeling.

Pupation

That's your name, Justin. Why aren't you standing up? I think. My whole body feels frozen stiff, even down to my toes. I can't stop myself from staring at my hands. *Great, here you are embarrassing yourself,* I think. My heart pounds louder and louder in my ears. My body starts to feel really strange.

"Whoa, what's happening to Justin's arms?" one of my classmates asks.

"Is that, like, an exoskeleton?" asks another.

I try to scream as I watch a brown shell slowly encase my whole body, but no sound comes out of my mouth.

1. What adjective does the narrator use to describe how his body feels?
   - (A) louder
   - (B) frozen
   - (C) standing
   - (D) heavy

2. Which word best describes how Justin is feeling at the end of this text?
   - (A) bored
   - (B) curious
   - (C) shocked
   - (D) excited

3. Why is some of the text in italics?
   - (A) It shows what the character is thinking.
   - (B) It shows what the character is saying.
   - (C) It shows what the character is feeling.
   - (D) It shows when the character is yelling.

4. What is another word or phrase for *encase*?
   - (A) squeeze
   - (B) pull down
   - (C) wrap around
   - (D) shake

Name: ______________________________ Date: ______________

Directions: Read the text, and answer the questions.

As You Read

Put a ! next to things you find surprising or interesting.

Ready to Present

The whole class is silent. My body has become a huge chrysalis. Mr. Lopez is about to call for help, when suddenly—RI-I-I-IP! I claw the chrysalis open and step out of it like a pair of pants.

"That's *disgusting*," says a boy named Antonio.

I am covered in slime. My friend Nalu offers me a jacket. I apologize before I use it to wipe my hands and face. I stretch my neck and roll my shoulders. When I look at my hands, I'm relieved to find I'm still human.

But my back feels strange and heavy. I stretch my arms, and two sets of brightly colored wings unfurl on my back.

1. Which phrase is an example of a simile?
   - (A) stretch my neck and roll my shoulders
   - (B) wings unfurl on my back
   - (C) covered in slime
   - (D) step out of it like a pair of pants

2. What comes out of the narrator's back?
   - (A) wings
   - (B) tentacles
   - (C) arms
   - (D) butterflies

3. Explain how you know this story is fantasy.

   ____

   ____

4. Write a prediction about what you think will happen next in the story.

   ____

Name: ______________________________ Date: ______________

As You Read

Put a ! next to things you find surprising or interesting.

The Presentation

I quickly fold my wings against my back again. I don't want to hit anyone in the face. I grab my poster and rush to the front of the room. Everyone is looking at me. But something about my wings makes me feel so confident, and I forget to feel nervous.

"So, I guess I should start by saying that my project is about butterflies," I say. "The Cairns birdwing butterfly. As you can see, the males have black, yellow, and green wings. Females are slightly bigger, and their wings are black, yellow, and white."

A girl asks, "Do chrysalises turn into butterflies as fast as you did?"

"I'm glad you asked. And I'm glad that my chrysalis stage happened so fast! Cairns birdwings take about a month to come out of their chrysalises. Then, it takes a few hours for their wings to dry. Mine feel dry already, though," I say as I stretch out my brilliant wings.

Another student raises a hand. "Justin, can you fly?"

"I don't know, and I'm going to finish presenting before I try," I answer. "Does anyone have any other questions about butterflies?" Three hands wave frantically in the air, and I call on the first one I see.

One classmate asks, "Where can I find one of these butterflies?"

"Cairns birdwing butterflies live in Australia," I reply.

Another asks, "What do they eat?"

I say, "Just like all butterflies, they love eating flower nectar. They have super long tongues to suck out nectar."

The last classmate asks, "Are those two wings, or four?"

"Well, I do have two forewings," I say with a laugh. I realize I need to explain my joke. "The two big wings that stretch past a butterfly's head are forewings. The two small wings that stretch past the abdomen are hindwings." I flutter my wings to demonstrate. All of a sudden, they crumble against my shirt. Black, yellow, and green dust shimmers, then disappears. I pause, but I keep presenting my project, just like I'd practiced. My classmates don't seem to mind. They're still listening. When I'm done, they cheer so loud my ears ring.

Name: ______________________________ Date: ______________

Directions: Read "The Presentation." Then, answer the questions.

1. How do the wings make Justin feel?

Ⓐ confused
Ⓑ scared
Ⓒ nervous
Ⓓ confident

2. What does the adverb *frantically* tell you about the students in the class?

Ⓐ They already know a lot about Cairns birdwing butterflies.
Ⓑ They really want to ask Justin some questions.
Ⓒ They are not interested in Justin's presentation.
Ⓓ They are excited to give their own presentations.

3. What happens to the narrator's wings in the end?

Ⓐ They turn to dust and disappear.
Ⓑ They grow bigger and bigger.
Ⓒ They change colors.
Ⓓ They fly away.

4. Where does Justin say the Cairns birdwing butterfly lives?

Ⓐ America
Ⓑ Australia
Ⓒ Africa
Ⓓ Antarctica

5. Describe the beginning, middle, and end of the story.

Beginning	Middle	End

Name: ______________________________ Date: ______________

Directions: Reread "The Presentation." Then, respond to the prompt.

Think of a different insect the main character could become. Explain how the story would be different.

____

____

____

____

____

____

____

____

____

____

____

____

____

Name: ______________________ Date: ____________

Zebra Longwing Diagrams

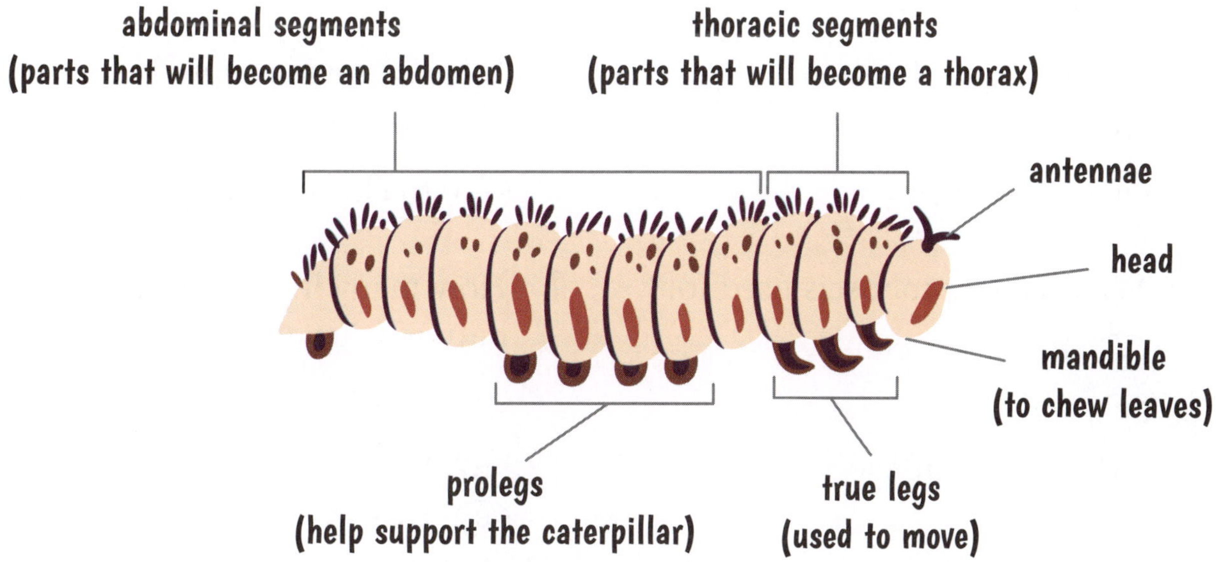

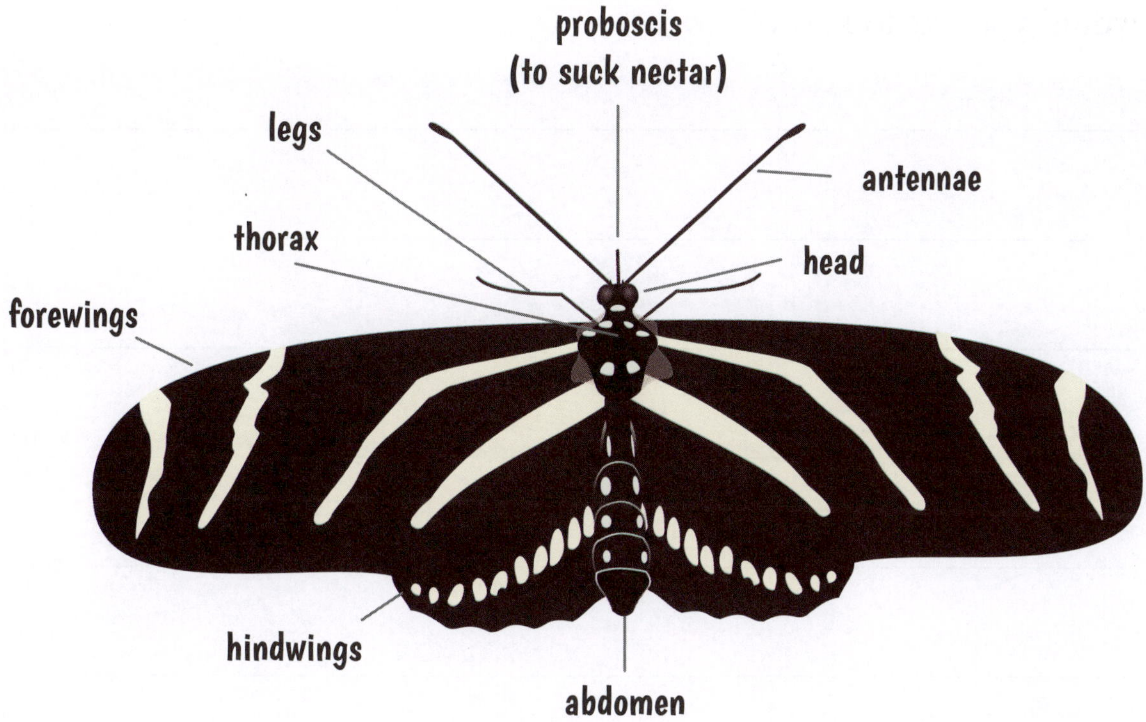

Name: ______________________________ Date: ______________

Directions: Read "Zebra Longwing Diagrams." Then, answer the questions.

1. Where would you most likely find this text?
   - (A) a newspaper
   - (B) a science textbook
   - (C) a book of short stories
   - (D) a dictionary

2. What is the proboscis used for?
   - (A) to suck nectar
   - (B) to fly
   - (C) to camouflage
   - (D) to land

3. What is the function of the caterpillar's true legs?
   - (A) to move
   - (B) to provide support
   - (C) to suck nectar
   - (D) to chew leaves

4. How many hindwings does the butterfly have?
   - (A) three
   - (B) one
   - (C) two
   - (D) five

5. What other information might be helpful in these diagrams? What else would you like to know?

____

____

____

____

____

____

____

____

Name: ______________________________ Date: ______________

Directions: Closely read these texts. Visualize what the texts are describing. Then, draw pictures to show what you visualize from each of the texts.

Close-Reading Texts

The Delicate Lives of Monarch Butterflies	Ready to Present
Monarchs migrate from a summer to a winter habitat. They may be the only butterfly species to do this. Most start their migration in September or October. They travel the same routes each year. Their journey is divided by many stops. Each night, monarchs stop to rest or feed. They gather in a tree. This may be a eucalyptus tree. It could be a pine or a cypress. A single tree can have thousands of monarchs in it.	I am covered in slime. My friend Nalu offers me a jacket. I apologize before I use it to wipe my hands and face. I stretch my neck and roll my shoulders. When I look down at my hands, I'm relieved to find I'm still human. But my back feels strange and heavy. I stretch my arms, and two sets of brightly colored wings unfurl on my back.

The Delicate Lives of Monarch Butterflies	Ready to Present

Name: ______________________ Date: ______________

Directions: Closely read these texts. Study the diagrams on page 131. Then, compare and contrast the Cairns birdwing butterfly with the zebra longwing butterfly.

Close-Reading Texts

Excerpt 1 from "The Presentation"	Excerpt 2 from "The Presentation"
"So, I guess I should start by saying that my project is about butterflies," I say. "The Cairns birdwing butterfly. As you can see, the males have black, yellow, and green wings. Females are slightly bigger, and their wings are black, yellow, and white."	Another asks, "What do they eat?" I say, "Just like all butterflies, they love eating flower nectar. They have super long tongues to suck out nectar." The last classmate asks, "Are those two wings, or four?" "Well, I do have two forewings," I say with a laugh. I realize I need to explain my joke. "The two big wings that stretch past a butterfly's head are forewings. The two small wings that stretch past the abdomen are hindwings."

Cairns Birdwing Butterfly	Zebra Longwing Butterfly

Both

Name: ______________________________ Date: ______________

Directions: Think about the texts from this unit. Then, respond to the prompt.

Imagine you are a butterfly. Describe your typical day. Use sequence words to show the order of things that happen in your day.

Name: ______________________________ Date: ______________

Directions: Choose an insect you find interesting. It can be a butterfly or something different. Do some research. Draw and label a diagram of the insect you chose.

Name: ______________________________ Date: ______________

Directions: Read the text, and answer the questions.

As You Read

Underline reasons the author gives for speaking different languages.

Speaking New Languages

People around the world speak different languages. Each region has its own native language. Some people learn to speak more than one language. They may need one language to talk with family or friends. They may require another language for school or work. Or they may learn a new language so they can travel to a new place. Learning to speak new languages can be a lot of fun!

1. Which word summarizes the topic of this text?

- (A) native
- (B) language
- (C) learning
- (D) people

2. What is a synonym for the word *learn*?

- (A) hate
- (B) hit
- (C) help
- (D) gain

3. Which word from the text could have an *–ly* added to make a new word?

- (A) learn
- (B) require
- (C) work
- (D) new

4. What does the phrase *native language* mean in the text?

- (A) the language of a child
- (B) the language of a specific place
- (C) the language of animals
- (D) the language of nature

Unit 8
WEEK 1
DAY
2

Name: ______________________ Date: ______________

Directions: Read the text, and answer the questions.

As You Read

Underline reasons the author gives to tell why global warming is a problem.

Harm from Global Warming

Global warming is a big problem. As the planet warms, glaciers melt. This causes the ocean waters to rise. Some towns are right on the coasts. Whole countries in the polar regions have or are near glaciers. People who live near coasts are nervous about the water levels. Their towns could be covered by water someday. Melting glaciers are also a problem for animals that live near them. Their homes are changing. Many people are doing what they can to reverse these changes.

A glacier melts in Iceland.

1. Which phrase from the text tells a reader most about this text?

- (A) glaciers melt
- (B) right on the coast
- (C) reverse these changes
- (D) global warming is a big problem

2. Which word has the same root word as *doing*?

- (A) dong
- (B) doable
- (C) donut
- (D) going

3. Which is **not** a synonym for *entire*?

- (A) complete
- (B) part
- (C) whole
- (D) full

4. What does the phrase *to reverse these changes* mean?

- (A) fix the problem
- (B) move backward
- (C) spin around
- (D) give money

Name: ______________________________ Date: ________________

Directions: Read the text, and answer the questions.

As You Read

Underline words or phrases that describe nature preserves.

Protection at Nature Preserves

A nature preserve is an area of land or water. It is set aside for wildlife. People cannot build or develop there. No hunting or fishing is allowed. Preserves are safe places for wildlife to live. They help species that are dying out. They protect endangered species. People are allowed to visit some of these areas. They have to follow the rules. There are nature preserves all over the world.

1. What is the text about?
   - (A) This text describes where nature preserves are located.
   - (B) This text describes why nature preserves are so important.
   - (C) This text describes why nature preserves do not work.
   - (D) This text describes why nature preserves are the same as national parks.

2. What does the phrase *dying out* mean in this text?
   - (A) moving away
   - (B) becoming extinct
   - (C) dying quickly
   - (D) going outside

3. What do people hope is the effect of nature preserves?

   ____

4. Would you visit a nature preserve? Why or why not?

   ____

   ____

Name: ______________________ Date: ______________

As You Read

Put stars next to details you think show Iceland is unique or interesting.

Iceland

Iceland is a country in Europe. It is a special place for many reasons. First, it is in a unique part of the world. Iceland is the most western country in Europe. It is a small island. It is completely surrounded by water. The capital is Reykjavík (REY-kyuh-veek).

Not many people live in Iceland. But they are proud people. They are proud of their culture and traditions. People in Iceland speak Icelandic. Some of them also learn English.

The landscape of Iceland is remarkable. Part of the island is covered in glacial ice. Some of the coastline was created by fjords (fee-ORDs). These are deep inlets. Small or narrow bays of water are found here. They were carved by glaciers.

Iceland is a volcanic island. There are many volcanoes there. There have been recent eruptions. The last big one was in 2010. It blew ash into the sky. Smoke filled the air. It was hard for planes to fly around Europe.

People in Iceland take care of their beautiful land. There are national parks. There are also many nature preserves. These areas are protected. The plants and animals are protected as well. This includes reindeer! The Arctic fox is also found in Iceland. It is the only land animal native to Iceland. These foxes are also protected.

The love of the land is shown in Iceland's flag. The flag includes three colors. The colors are symbols. There is red. This stands for the island's volcanic fire. There is also white. This stands for snow and ice. Finally, there is blue. This stands for the ocean that surrounds the land.

Name: ______________________________ Date: ______________

Directions: Read "Iceland." Then, answer the questions.

1. Which prediction is based on the title and image?
   - (A) The text is about an icy land.
   - (B) The text is about icy weather.
   - (C) The text is about the country of Iceland.
   - (D) The text is about mapping.

2. What is the author's purpose?
   - (A) to share information about maps
   - (B) to give opinions about life in Iceland
   - (C) to persuade readers to love volcanoes
   - (D) to share information about Iceland

3. Which statement shows prior knowledge related to the text?
   - (A) I saw a reindeer in my Christmas book.
   - (B) I have seen a picture of fjords in Iceland.
   - (C) I have seen many different maps before.
   - (D) This text reminds me that my family speaks Spanish and English.

4. Which detail describes the unique landscape in Iceland?
   - (A) The flag includes three colors.
   - (B) Reindeer are found in Iceland.
   - (C) Part of the island is covered in glacial ice.
   - (D) Icelanders speak Icelandic.

5. Write details from the text that support the main idea.

Detail	**Detail**
Main Idea Iceland is a fascinating and unique country.	
Detail	**Detail**

Name: ______________________ Date: ____________

Directions: Reread "Iceland." Then, respond to the prompt.

Think about the things that make Iceland unique and special. What connections can you make between Iceland and another place? Compare and contrast Iceland with this other place. How are they similar? How are they different?

Name: ______________________________ Date: ______________

Directions: Read the text, and answer the questions.

As You Read

Underline words or phrases that tell you about the setting.

A Fox Alone

Arctic Fox used to be alone in Iceland. Not totally alone, of course. She had all the birds and fish she could get her paws on. But Arctic Fox was once the only mammal to walk this land of ice. She found peace in her loneliness. She could drink all the rivers by herself. She could tear apart birds' nests and feast on the tasty little eggs inside. And, most importantly, she could frolic in the white, silent snow. Then, a bit more than a thousand years ago, a new kind of mammal joined Arctic Fox. This was the first of many changes.

1. What is the setting?

- (A) Iceland
- (B) Greenland
- (C) Antarctica
- (D) New Zealand

2. Which word best describes how Arctic Fox feels?

- (A) annoyed
- (B) peaceful
- (C) anxious
- (D) scared

3. When does this story take place?

- (A) long ago
- (B) in the present
- (C) in the future
- (D) a few years ago

4. What is the meaning of the word *feast* in the text?

- (A) eat
- (B) a large meal
- (C) hunt
- (D) drink

Name: ______________________ Date: ______________

Directions: Read the text, and answer the questions.

As You Read

Put a ? next to anything that is confusing or that makes you wonder something.

More Mammals Arrive

This new mammal was known as the Human Being, and it built its house in the forest. The chimney spewed hazy black smoke all night and day. The Human Being was not alone. It brought friends like Dog, Cow, Horse, Sheep, and Reindeer. These animals trampled over the moss and ate up every blade of grass.

"They all smell disgusting," growled Arctic Fox. "Though I am grateful for that plump, tasty Chicken." She plucked a feather out of her fangs.

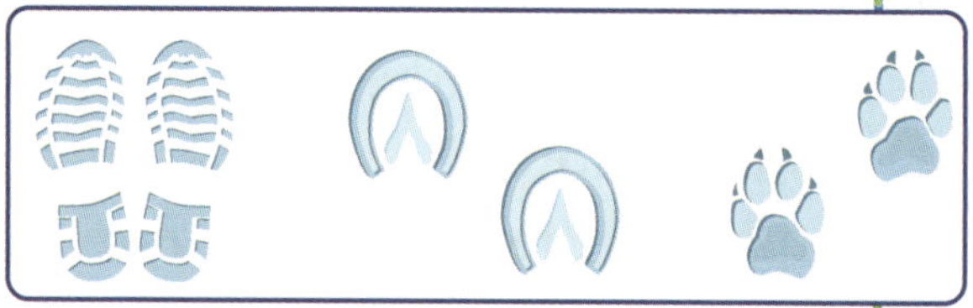

1. Which word best describes how Arctic Fox feels about Human Being?
   - (A) fearful
   - (B) annoyed
   - (C) curious
   - (D) uninterested

2. Which word is spelled correctly?
   - (A) greateful
   - (B) graitfull
   - (C) greatful
   - (D) grateful

3. How do readers know that Arctic Fox ate Chicken?
   - (A) She eats up the grass.
   - (B) She has feathers in her teeth.
   - (C) She tells Human Being that she did.
   - (D) The animals cannot find Chicken.

4. What is another way to say *trampled over*?
   - (A) stomped on
   - (B) pulled out
   - (C) broke apart
   - (D) slid across

Name: ______________________________ Date: ______________

Directions: Read the text, and answer the questions.

As You Read

Put a ? next to anything that is confusing or that makes you wonder something.

Rodent Refreshments

The Human Being also brought foes, including Mouse and Rat. The Human Being hated these rodents. It did not mean to bring the pests, but they hitched a ride in Human Being's coat pockets. Mouse and Rat ate up the harvest and dug holes through the house.

Arctic Fox, on the other hand, was grateful for Mouse and Rat. She decided she quite liked the taste of rodent meat.

"I can learn to live with this Human Being," she decided. "I still have plenty of space and plenty of quiet. Plus, I'm glad to eat Mouse, Rat, and Chicken."

But then, the Human Being brought one more creature that Arctic Fox just couldn't stand.

1. Why is Arctic Fox grateful for Mouse and Rat?
   - (A) They give her gifts.
   - (B) They leave her alone.
   - (C) They are her good friends.
   - (D) She likes to eat them.

2. The title of the text is an example of ______.
   - (A) alliteration
   - (B) personification
   - (C) a metaphor
   - (D) hyperbole

3. How do Mouse and Rat get to Iceland?

   ____

   ____

4. Write a prediction about what you think will happen next.

   ____

   ____

   ____

Name: ______________________ Date: ____________

As You Read

Put a ? next to anything that is confusing or that makes you wonder something.

Fox and Mink in Iceland

The Human Being wanted a fine fur coat to keep warm. So, it brought the sleek Mink to Iceland. The Human Being kept Mink locked in a cage.

"You'll look lovely on me," laughed the Human Being.

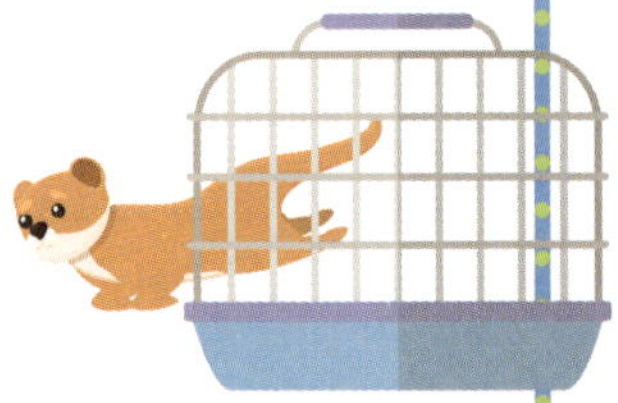

"You'll never make a coat out of me," cried Mink. He waited until the Human Being turned its back. Then, he slipped through the bars of his cage. Mink scampered out of the house and into Chicken's coop. Then, he sucked up each one of Chicken's eggs.

When Arctic Fox arrived, she couldn't believe her eyes. "Who are you, revolting slob? You've eaten up my dinner," she snapped.

"I apologize. I didn't know anyone else ate these things," said Mink.

Just then, Human Being burst into the barn. "Now I've got you," it cried as it threw a net over Mink and Arctic Fox. Mink wriggled through the net and hid in a hole. Arctic Fox struggled and gnashed her teeth, but she couldn't break free. So, Human Being locked her in a cage.

"This is your fault," Arctic Fox shouted at Mink. "You, Human Being, and all the other beasts it brought into Iceland have ruined everything!"

"Human Being locked me in a cage, too," said Mink. "I lived every day terrified of being turned into a coat."

"You escaped, though," Arctic Fox replied. "You're so nimble, I bet you could easily open my cage." Mink felt flattered, so he agreed to free Arctic Fox. As soon as he did so, Arctic Fox lunged at Mink.

"I'll make you my dinner so you can't steal more food," she growled.

"There's plenty of delicious food for both of us, don't you think? We can hunt together or stick to our own areas," Mink spluttered.

"I prefer to be alone," said Arctic Fox, and her jaw opened wide.

Mink made a last desperate attempt to save himself. "What if the Human Being catches you again? I'm the only one who can help," he said.

Arctic Fox realized he was right. "The peace and quiet I once knew is gone," she sighed. "I want to live peacefully. I'd rather have an ally than a competitor." She loosened her grip, and Mink ran into the wilderness.

Arctic Fox and Mink didn't talk much after that. But whenever they were in need, they could always count on each other.

Name: ______________________________ Date: ______________

Directions: Read "Fox and Mink in Iceland." Then, answer the questions.

1. Which statement best describes the relationship between Arctic Fox and Mink at the end of the text?

- (A) They are competitors.
- (B) They are best friends and allies.
- (C) They are enemies.
- (D) They are allies but not close friends.

2. How does Mink help Arctic Fox?

- (A) Mink brings her fresh eggs.
- (B) Mink catches food for her.
- (C) Mink frees her from the cage.
- (D) Mink helps her find a home.

3. Which word explains how a character moved?

- (A) growled
- (B) scampered
- (C) shouted
- (D) snapped

4. Who are the main characters?

- (A) Arctic Fox and Mink
- (B) Mink and Human Being
- (C) Arctic Fox and Human Being
- (D) Arctic Fox and Chicken

5. Compare and contrast Arctic Fox and Mink from the story.

Arctic Fox	Both	Mink

Name: ______________________________ Date: ______________

Directions: Reread "Fox and Mink in Iceland." Then, respond to the prompt.

Imagine Arctic Fox and Mink meet up with each other today. Write a dialogue that might occur between the two animals.

Name: ______________________ Date: ____________

Icelandic Penpal

New Message

To: Brichelle

Subject: Hello (Halló) From Iceland!

Dear Brichelle,

Writing to you has been lovely! I'm excited to get to know someone from the United States.

In your last letter, you asked what things we do differently here in Iceland. For one, our last names are different from yours. In most countries, last names are passed down for generations. But in Iceland, most people's last names are their father's first name. Then, you add -sson for boys or -dottir for girls. Today, women sometimes give their kids their own names. My mother Hrefna did that. Therefore, my name is Fannar Hrefnasson because I am her son. My sister is named Björn Hrefnadottir. Last names can get confusing. That's why we call everyone by their first name. Even teachers and the president!

Another big difference here is the sun. In the summer, the sun hardly ever goes down. Everyone stays up past midnight. It's just too hard to sleep through all that sunlight. In the winter, the sun takes ages to come up. My sister and I go sledding every day in the winter. It's important to stay busy when it's dark out. Winter here can make people feel sad. To stay cheerful, we exercise and talk to each other.

These are two big differences between our countries. But your life in Maine is not so different from mine in Iceland. We are both familiar with cold and storms. We both have younger sisters, and we both go to school. Also, I take piano lessons, just like you! What other things do we have in common? How do you like to spend your dark winter days?

Sincerely,
Fannar Hrefnasson

Name: ____________________ Date: ____________

Directions: Read "Icelandic Penpal." Then, answer the questions.

1. Where does Brichelle live?

- (A) Iceland
- (B) Maine
- (C) Australia
- (D) California

2. The text is an example of _____.

- (A) a short story
- (B) a text message
- (C) a written letter
- (D) an email

3. Which word means "hello" in Icelandic?

- (A) Halló
- (B) Hola
- (C) Bonjour
- (D) 'Ahlan

4. *Sincerely, Fannar Hrefnasson* is an example of ______.

- (A) a subject of a letter or email
- (B) a greeting of a letter or email
- (C) a closing of a letter or email
- (D) a heading of a letter or email

5. How are Fannar and Brichelle similar? Write one or two examples.

____

____

____

____

____

____

____

____

Name: ______________________ Date: ____________

Directions: Closely read these texts. Visualize what the texts say. Then, draw pictures to show what you visualize from each of the texts. Answer the question.

Close-Reading Texts

Iceland	A Fox Alone
The landscape of Iceland is remarkable. Part of the island is covered in glacial ice. Some of the coastline was created by fjords (fee-ORDs). These are deep inlets. Small or narrow bays of water are found here. They were carved by glaciers. Iceland is a volcanic island. There are many volcanoes there. There have been recent eruptions.	Arctic Fox used to be alone in Iceland. Not totally alone, of course. She had all the birds and fish she could get her paws on. But Arctic Fox was once the only mammal to walk this land of ice. She found peace in her loneliness. She could drink all the rivers by herself. She could tear apart birds' nests and feast on the tasty little eggs inside. And, most importantly, she could frolic in the white, silent snow.

Iceland	A Fox Alone

What is one way your pictures are similar?

____

____

Unit 8
WEEK 3
DAY
3

Name: ______________________ Date: ____________

Directions: Closely read these texts. Write a dialogue the author of "Iceland" may have had with Fannar Hrefnasson related to Iceland.

Close-Reading Texts

Iceland	Icelandic Penpal
People in Iceland take care of their beautiful land. There are national parks. There are also many nature preserves. These areas are protected. The plants and animals are protected as well. This includes reindeer! The Arctic fox is also found in Iceland. It is the only land animal native to Iceland. These foxes are also protected.	Another big difference here is the sun. In the summer, the sun hardly ever goes down. Everyone stays up past midnight. It's just too hard to sleep through all that sunlight. In the winter, the sun takes ages to come up. My sister and I go sledding every day in the winter. It's important to stay busy when it's dark out. Winter here can make people feel sad. To stay cheerful, we exercise and talk to each other.

Name: ______________________________ Date: ________________

Directions: Think about the texts from this unit. Then, respond to the prompt.

Write a short story that takes place in Iceland. Make sure it has a beginning, middle, and end. Draw a picture to go with your story.

Name: ______________________ Date: ____________

Directions: Write an email response to Fannar. Answer his questions. Ask him some questions you have about Iceland. Tell him some interesting things about your life and where you live.

New Message

To:

Subject:

Name: ______________________ Date: ______________

Directions: Read the text, and answer the questions.

As You Read

Put a ? next to things that are confusing or that make you wonder about new things. Write your questions in the margins.

Sacagawea's Contribution

Sacagawea played a big role in history. She was an American Indian. She made a trip with Lewis and Clark. They were famous explorers. Most people believe she joined them because of her husband. He was a translator who worked for the group. And the group needed help speaking with other tribes. Sacagawea helped, too. She knew the land. She could also speak to other tribes. Her work helped the group make trades and find food.

Sacagawea standing with Lewis and Clark

1. Who is this text mostly about?
   - (A) Lewis
   - (B) Sacagawea
   - (C) Clark
   - (D) American Indians

2. Which word could add the prefix *dis–* to make another word?
   - (A) group
   - (B) speak
   - (C) believe
   - (D) food

3. What is another form of the verb *speaking*?
   - (A) speeding
   - (B) talking
   - (C) peak
   - (D) spoke

4. Which word describes the tone of this text?
   - (A) informative
   - (B) silly
   - (C) funny
   - (D) romantic

Name: ______________________ Date: ______________

Directions: Read the text, and answer the questions.

As You Read

Put a ? next to things that are confusing or that make you wonder about new things. Write your questions in the margins.

Observations by Lewis and Clark

Lewis and Clark learned so much about the land in the region. They observed many new plants and animals. They gathered facts about these new species. They brought that information home with them. They wanted to share it with others. Lewis and Clark were the first Europeans to discover the magpie bird. They saw these birds in 1804.

magpie bird

1. Which statement shows a strong connection to the text?
   - (A) Mrs. Lewis is my piano teacher.
   - (B) I think pigeons are annoying.
   - (C) I like to notice things in nature like Lewis and Clark did.
   - (D) I want a new pet animal in my home.

2. What is the subject of the first sentence from the text?
   - (A) Lewis
   - (B) Lewis and Clark
   - (C) Clark
   - (D) region

3. Which word is a synonym for *gathered*?
   - (A) compared
   - (B) argued
   - (C) noticed
   - (D) collected

4. What does the language tell you about the author's purpose?
   - (A) The language is personal so people will feel like they know Lewis and Clark.
   - (B) The language is factual so people will learn more about Lewis and Clark.
   - (C) The language is funny so people will laugh about Lewis and Clark.
   - (D) The language is persuasive so people will believe things about Lewis and Clark.

Name: ______________________________ **Date:** ______________

Directions: Read the text, and answer the questions.

As You Read

Put a ! next to things you think are important or interesting.

Thomas Jefferson Sends Groups West

Thomas Jefferson was the third president. He had dreams of exploring the West. For years, he tried to find a way to organize a group to explore. Lewis and Clark were one group he sent to gather facts about the new land. He ordered other groups to other parts of the country. He wanted the group to explore all the way to the West Coast. Many years later, that is what happened.

President Thomas Jefferson

1. Which index entry would best help a reader find this information?
   - (A) Jefferson at war
   - (B) Jefferson's family life
   - (C) role of Jefferson in expedition
   - (D) Jefferson's childhood

2. What does the phrase *that is what happened* refer to?
   - (A) Thomas Jefferson died.
   - (B) The group explored the West Coast.
   - (C) Thomas Jefferson explored the West himself.
   - (D) Thomas Jefferson met Lewis and Clark.

3. What is the root word in *exploring*?

____

4. What other photo or image would you add to this text? What could readers learn from it?

____

____

Name: ________________________ Date: ______________

As You Read

Write questions or thoughts you have about the text or image in the margins.

Lewis and Clark

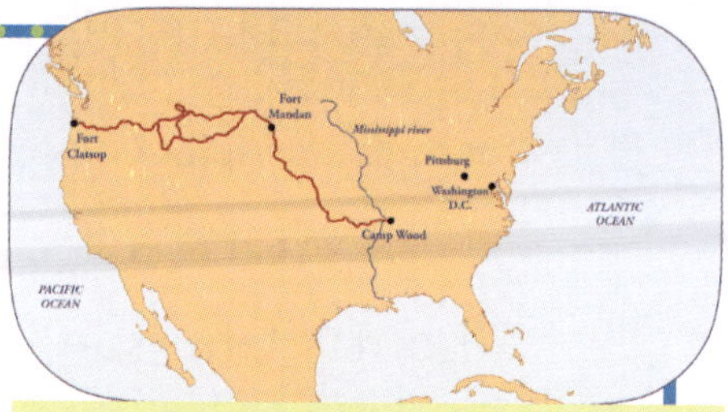

map of the Lewis and Clark expedition

More than 200 years ago, European people did not know a lot about the western part of the United States. Going west was an exciting adventure. It was also a difficult journey.

Two famous explorers made that trip. They were named Meriwether Lewis and William Clark. They traveled when little was known to Europeans about the West. There were no maps to show them the way. Their goal was to reach the Pacific Ocean.

Lewis and Clark began their journey in 1804. It was not just the two of them on their trip. They had many people to help them. More than 40 people joined Lewis and Clark. They packed a lot of food and supplies for their whole group.

Lewis and Clark kept good records of their journey. They both wrote detailed records of where they went. Clark made maps. The maps showed the route they took as well as the rivers and mountains they crossed. Lewis wrote in a journal about their journey and the places they stayed. He also included information about plants and animals they saw.

Many American Indians helped Lewis and Clark. They worked as guides to show them where to go. They also helped the group find food and other supplies.

Lewis and Clark finally reached the ocean shore. They had traveled for more than a year. They were thrilled to see the Pacific Ocean. They were also eager to go home.

The group knew going back to Missouri would be a long trip. So, they spent the winter at a place called Fort Clatsop. This area is in Oregon. After about six months, the group began the journey home.

Lewis and Clark taught people about what they found. Their stories and maps were very helpful for people who traveled west. Lewis and Clark's journey took them an entire year, but today, it would only take a few hours on an airplane. A lot has changed since their time!

Name: ______________________ Date: ______________

Directions: Read "Lewis and Clark." Then, answer the questions.

1. What is the most important idea from the text about Lewis and Clark?

- (A) They learned about the West and shared with others.
- (B) They traveled slowly and did not have maps.
- (C) They traveled in three boats with many people.
- (D) They wanted to reach the Pacific Ocean.

2. Which statement shows a strong connection to the text?

- (A) I do not like to go on boats.
- (B) I have always wanted to explore new places.
- (C) I know there are seven oceans.
- (D) I live in the state of Texas.

3. What is the author's purpose?

- (A) to teach people about geography
- (B) to inform people about Lewis and Clark
- (C) to teach people about American Indians
- (D) to entertain people with a story

4. What did Lewis and Clark share about their trip?

- (A) how to navigate a boat
- (B) ways to survive the trip in the winter
- (C) animals and plants in the West
- (D) how to survive the heat of the summer months

5. Write four major events in Lewis and Clark's expedition. Write them in the order they occurred.

Event 1	
Event 2	
Event 3	
Event 4	

Name: ______________________ Date: ______________

Directions: Reread "Lewis and Clark." Then, respond to the prompt.

What do you think it would have been like to travel with Lewis and Clark? Write about what the expedition would have been like for you. Draw a picture of yourself on the trail.

Name: ______________________________ Date: ________________

Directions: Read the text, and answer the questions.

As You Read

Put a ? next to anything that is confusing, such as an unfamiliar word. Write questions or thoughts in the margins.

November 4, 1804

My husband Toussaint met two men today. They're explorers named Meriwether Lewis and William Clark. They are staying here at Fort Mandan for the winter. Toussaint wants both of us to help them on their journey. The explorers need someone who can translate the Shoshone language. Toussaint thinks I'm perfect for the job.

But I'm currently pregnant. So, by the time the expedition leaves in April, I'll have a baby with me. I asked why these men couldn't hire anyone else. Toussaint insisted there was no one else. He said it was fine for the baby and me to come with him. So, in a few months, the three of us will follow these men into the wilderness.

1. Where does this story begin?

Ⓐ Fort Mandan
Ⓑ Toussaint's house
Ⓒ the wilderness
Ⓓ a Shoshone village

2. Who is most likely the narrator of this text?

Ⓐ Meriwether Lewis
Ⓑ William Clark
Ⓒ Toussaint, Sacagawea's husband
Ⓓ Sacagawea

3. When does this story take place?

Ⓐ present day
Ⓑ the fall of 1804
Ⓒ the summer of 1804
Ⓓ the winter in the distant future

4. What is a definition of *expedition*?

Ⓐ a person who can translate a language
Ⓑ a wilderness area with few people
Ⓒ a group of people on a journey to explore
Ⓓ a village of people that work together

Name: ______________________________ Date: ________________

Directions: Read the text, and answer the questions.

As You Read

Try making connections to the text—to yourself, the world, or another text. Write a ∞ wherever you make connections.

February 11, 1805

Jean Baptiste is my dear first child. He took his time coming into the world. No medicine could ease the pain that wracked my body. But finally, my son was here. He heaved a breath deep into his belly and bellowed out his first cry. I held him close and soothed him with the rising and falling of my chest. We fell asleep together as the evening sun sank.

Jean Baptiste is strong, I can see that already. His tiny fingers grasp at the air, and his curious eyes drink in everything. This is a child who can travel the world with me. He will do well on our journey.

1. Who is Jean Baptiste?
   - Ⓐ the narrator's baby
   - Ⓑ the narrator's brother
   - Ⓒ the narrator's husband
   - Ⓓ the narrator's friend

2. What does the author mean by the phrase *his curious eyes drink in everything*?
   - Ⓐ He cries a lot.
   - Ⓑ He looks at and notices everything.
   - Ⓒ He is always hungry or thirsty.
   - Ⓓ He has trouble seeing clearly.

3. What is a synonym for *shouted*?
   - Ⓐ soothed
   - Ⓑ grasped
   - Ⓒ bellowed
   - Ⓓ heaved

4. What is an antonym for *curious*?
   - Ⓐ odd
   - Ⓑ uninterested
   - Ⓒ nosy
   - Ⓓ adventurous

Name: ______________________ Date: ______________

Directions: Read the text, and answer the questions.

As You Read

Underline things in the text you find interesting or important.

August 14, 1805

Lewis and Clark have split up the party. Toussaint, my husband, and I will head to a fork in the river. Lewis took a smaller group of men to a Shoshone camp. He wants to ask these Shoshone what the land ahead is like. I want to ask, too, and I'm eager to see another Shoshone person. But Lewis told me I should stay here and keep my baby safe. He's worried that this group of Shoshone may be hostile. I don't see how anyone could be hostile to me and my sweet Jean Baptiste, though. My boy charms everyone he meets with his smile.

1. Which is a strong conclusion from this text?

- (A) She has never seen a Shoshone person.
- (B) She is also from the Shoshone tribe.
- (C) There are many Shoshone people with her.
- (D) She does not like Shoshone people.

2. Which word from the text describes a feeling?

- (A) worried
- (B) hostile
- (C) safe
- (D) charms

3. What is meant by the phrase *a fork in the river*? Use words or pictures to explain it.

4. Do you think Sacagawea should go to the Shoshone camp? Why or why not?

____

____

____

Name: ______________________ Date: ______________

As You Read

Write a ∞ wherever you make connections.

August 17, 1805

At last, we set out to meet Lewis and the Shoshone people. I carried Jean Baptiste on my back. Suddenly, a few Shoshone men rode up on horseback. I saw the chief who led them, and I gasped aloud. It was none other than my brother, Cameahwait. I couldn't contain my joy, so I leapt and twirled. Jean Baptiste wriggled in his cradleboard. Cameahwait saw my frantic dancing, and he realized who I was. The moment our eyes met, I rushed to him and cried out, "Brother!" He dismounted and rushed into my arms. We laughed and wrapped each other in a warm embrace. His deerskin shirt smelled like home.

"Sacagawea," he cried out in disbelief. Though his firm posture never wavered, he seemed tired. His shoulders sagged, and his face looked thin. So much had happened since the last time I saw him. I had endless questions to ask him. I started with, "Brother, are you eating well?"

"No one has been eating well. The Hidatsa banned us from hunting," Cameahwait explained. "The only thing left to eat is berries."

He told me of their troubles with the Hidatsa tribe. The Hidatsa had guns, and the Shoshone couldn't fight back without their own guns.

"Lewis has arranged to send rifles," my brother said. "I've given him horses in exchange for his help. Until the guns arrive, we will survive on berries."

I squeezed my brother's hands tight. "Your stomach will be full tonight," I reassured him. "A hunter from the expedition party got a deer today."

"I hope you fill your stomach, too. You need strength for your baby," Cameahwait said.

I took Jean Baptiste out of his cradleboard. The babbling baby entertained his uncle all night. He kept grabbing onto his uncle's fingers, and Cameahwait laughed every time.

I'll be sad to leave my brother again. Seeing him has renewed my energy. All I can do is hope for his safety as my journey continues on.

Name: ______________________________ Date: ______________

Directions: Read "August 17, 1805." Then, answer the questions.

1. What genre of text is this?

Ⓐ poetry
Ⓑ nonfiction
Ⓒ fantasy
Ⓓ historical fiction

2. Who is Cameahwait?

Ⓐ the narrator's baby
Ⓑ the narrator's brother
Ⓒ the narrator's husband
Ⓓ the narrator's father

3. What is meant by the words *fill your stomach*?

Ⓐ eat enough food
Ⓑ drink a lot of water
Ⓒ have a tasty meal
Ⓓ do not eat too much

4. What reason does Cameahwait give for giving horses to Lewis?

Ⓐ They are in exchange for guns.
Ⓑ He borrows horses from him before.
Ⓒ They are in exchange for food.
Ⓓ Lewis pays him money for the horses.

5. Write details about the main character.

Character Analysis of the Narrator, Sacagawea	
Feelings	**Character Traits**
Relationship with Others	**Wants/Needs**

Name: ______________________________ Date: ______________

Directions: Reread the texts from this week. Then, respond to the prompt.

Imagine you are Sacagawea. Write the next entry in her journal. Choose a date for the entry. Describe how you are feeling. Write about things that are happening on your journey.

Name: ______________________ Date: ______________

Lewis and Clark Script

Lewis and Clark, Scene 4: The Barking Squirrel

Sgt. Ordoway: Look, another one popped out of its hole!

Lewis: What should we call these tiny creatures? Their bodies are shaped much like squirrels, but with shorter tails.

Clark: I think their body shape is more similar to a rat's.

Sgt. Ordoway: Its head is rounder than a rat's head. It looks to be a friendly little fellow, don't you think? Calling it a rat seems insulting.

Clark: Fine, then, a squirrel. It lives in the ground, so it shall be a burrowing squirrel.

Lewis: Try to say "burrowing squirrel" five times fast.

Clark: Burrowing squirrel, burrowing squirrel, burrowing squirrel, squirlow... hmm. Ground rat is much easier to say.

Lewis: Sure, but it's also much easier to forget.

Clark: If you've got so many wonderful ideas, why don't you name the animal?

Sgt. Ordoway: Shh, be quiet and listen. Do you hear the noises these creatures are making?

Clark: It sounds like they bark like little dogs when they're startled.

Lewis: That's it, a barking squirrel!

Sgt. Ordoway: No, I've got the perfect name—prairie dog. See, because they bark like dogs.

Clark: That's the silliest name I've ever heard. I'm sticking with ground rat.

Lewis: Barking squirrel, and that's final.

Sgt. Ordoway: Whatever you say.

Name: ______________________ Date: ____________

Directions: Read "Lewis and Clark Script." Then, answer the questions.

1. What is the tone of this text?

Ⓐ humorous
Ⓑ mysterious
Ⓒ romantic
Ⓓ informational

2. Why does Clark want to call the animal a burrowing squirrel?

Ⓐ It looks like a rat.
Ⓑ It barks like a dog.
Ⓒ It lives in the ground.
Ⓓ It climbs trees.

3. How does the animal the characters see look different from squirrels?

Ⓐ It has a shorter tail.
Ⓑ It has a longer tail.
Ⓒ It has more fur.
Ⓓ It has less fur.

4. Who wants to call the animal a ground rat?

Ⓐ Lewis
Ⓑ Clark
Ⓒ Sgt. Ordoway
Ⓓ Lewis and Clark

5. What do you think might happen in the next scene of this play?

____

____

____

____

____

____

____

____

Name: ______________________________ Date: ______________

Directions: Closely read these texts. Write a dialogue the authors may have had with each other related to Sacagawea.

Close-Reading Texts

Sacagawea's Contribution	November 4, 1804
Sacagawea played a big role in history. She was an American Indian. She made a trip with Lewis and Clark. They were famous explorers. Most people believe she joined them because of her husband. He was a translator who worked for the group. And the group needed help speaking with other tribes. Sacagawea helped, too. She knew the land. She could also speak to other tribes. Her work helped the group make trades and find food.	They're explorers named Meriwether Lewis and William Clark. They are staying here at Fort Mandan for the winter. Toussaint wants both of us to help them on their journey. The explorers need someone who can translate the Shoshone language. Toussaint thinks I'm perfect for the job. But I'm currently pregnant. So, by the time the expedition leaves in April, I'll have a baby with me. I asked why these men couldn't hire anyone else. Toussaint insisted there was no one else.

Name: ______________________ Date: ______________

Directions: Closely read this text. Then, study the script on page 167. Compare and contrast the two texts. Think about their purposes, tones, language, genres, and structures.

Close-Reading Text

Lewis and Clark	Lewis and Clark kept good records of their journey. They both wrote detailed records of where they went. Clark made maps. The maps showed the route they took as well as the rivers and mountains they crossed. Lewis wrote in a journal about their journey and the places they stayed. He also included information about plants and animals they saw.

Lewis and Clark

Both

Lewis and Clark Script

Name: ______________________________ Date: ____________

Directions: Think about the texts from this unit. Then, respond to the prompt.

Write a letter to one of the following people:

- Lewis
- Clark
- Sacagawea

Ask them some questions. Tell them what you think about their lives. Tell them some things about yourself.

______________________________,

____

____

____

____

____

____

____

____

____

______________________________,

____

Name: ______________________ Date: ______________

Directions: Write a script about you and a friend on an adventure. Try to make it humorous. Maybe you find a new animal like the characters from "Lewis and Clark Script." Maybe something else funny happens.

Name: ______________________________ Date: ________________

Directions: Read the text, and answer the questions.

As You Read

Put a ? next to anything that is confusing or that you have a question about. Share your questions with a partner.

Water Pressure

When swimmers dive deep, they may get a strange feeling in their ears. The water has put pressure on their eardrums. This does not happen in shallow water. So, why does water pressure increase with depth? Imagine weighing the water in the shallow end of a pool. Now, weigh the water in the deep end. The water in the deep end is much heavier because there is more of it. As divers go deeper, more and more water pushes them down.

1. Which of the statements is true?
   - (A) The deeper you go under water, the more pressure you feel.
   - (B) The water pressure stays the same at all depths.
   - (C) The deeper you go under water, the less pressure you feel.
   - (D) A short pool has less water pressure than a long pool.

2. Which is a compound word?
   - (A) eardrum
   - (B) pressure
   - (C) weighing
   - (D) strange

3. What can be an effect of diving down deep in the water?
   - (A) being able to see better underwater
   - (B) being able to swim faster
   - (C) feeling lighter
   - (D) getting a strange feeling in your ears

4. Which is an example of a prepositional phrase?
   - (A) weigh the water
   - (B) in shallow water
   - (C) pushes them down
   - (D) much heavier

Name: ______________________________ Date: ______________

Directions: Read the text, and answer the questions.

As You Read

Put a ? next to anything that is confusing or that you have a question about.

Giant Isopod

An armored, bug-like creature crawls across the ocean floor. It eats dead animals along the way. This beast is called a *giant isopod*. Giant isopods live in the deep sea. They are related to pill bugs. The resemblance is clear. Both animals have layers of gray armor on their backs. They can both curl up into balls, too.

Giant isopods are called "giant" for a reason. They can grow as long as 20 inches (50 centimeters). Their size means they are not built for speed. When giant isopods hunt for live food, they eat other slow animals. They also eat fish that humans have caught in traps.

1. What does the author compare giant isopods to?

Ⓐ deep sea
Ⓑ humans
Ⓒ fish
Ⓓ pill bugs

2. Which statement shows the best text-to-text connection?

Ⓐ I read a book about how to build a pool.
Ⓑ I read a book about scuba divers.
Ⓒ I read a book about fish that live in the deep sea.
Ⓓ I read a book about how humans catch fish.

3. What is the purpose of this text?

Ⓐ to entertain readers with a story
Ⓑ to inform readers about giant isopods
Ⓒ to persuade readers to catch giant isopods
Ⓓ to inform readers about pill bugs

4. What is the root word of *related*?

Ⓐ relate
Ⓑ late
Ⓒ ready
Ⓓ real

Name: ______________________ Date: ______________

Directions: Read the text, and answer the questions.

As You Read

Put a ! next to things you find interesting.

Bioluminescence

Some living things can light up. Their bodies have special chemicals in them. When they release the chemicals, a light goes off. This is bioluminescence. Creatures who light up are bioluminescent. This happens for different reasons. Lights can lure in a tasty meal. They can also startle a predator. Some creatures light up when they are touched. Creatures nearby can use that light. It allows them to find their way in the dark.

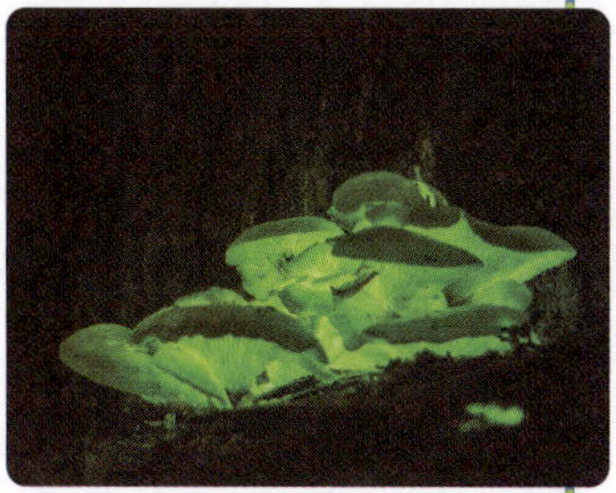

1. What causes bioluminescence?
   - (A) a light switch
   - (B) special chemicals
   - (C) water pressure
   - (D) breathing

2. What is another word for *startle*?
   - (A) release
   - (B) chase
   - (C) begin
   - (D) frighten

3. What is one reason some animals have bioluminescence?

____

____

4. Would you like to be able to light up at night? Why or why not?

____

____

____

Name: ______________________________ Date: ______________

As You Read

Put a ! next to things you think are the most important or interesting.

Deep Sea Creatures

anglerfish

Sunlight can shine through 660 feet (200 meters) of water. Below that, the light fades. The water gets colder. Plants cannot grow. This area is known as the *deep sea*. Some microbes and animals here are bioluminescent. Vampire squid have two ways of lighting up. They have bioluminescent organs on the tips of their eight arms. And if they get scared, their arms spit out a cloud of glowing mucus. The bright mucus can distract any predator.

Many deep sea fish have huge eyes. Their eyes can catch the faint light of other creatures. Crystal amphipods are one example. They look like see-through shrimp. They have large discs in their heads. Those discs are really their eyes. Their eyes are one-third of the length of their whole bodies! Barreleye fish are another example. They have jar-shaped eyes that point straight up. They can turn their eyes forward to search for prey. Barreleyes peek through their transparent heads.

Camouflage helps creatures hide from predators. It can also help them sneak up on prey. A few colors work well for deep sea camouflage. Many kinds of jellyfish and squid are almost fully transparent. Predators can look right through them. Anglerfish can be black to blend in with the darkness. Other kinds of anglerfish are red or pink. In the deep sea, the color red is invisible. This is because red light does not reach these depths. Transparent animals often have red organs. The red color hides the only visible part of their bodies.

Fish in the deep sea tend to be larger than fish from the shallows. They may also have very long lifespans. The world's largest bony fish lives in the deep sea. It is the giant oarfish. And the orange roughy is a fish that can live more than 200 years. Scientists do not know why animals can grow so big and so old here.

Living things in the deep sea have adapted to a cold, harsh life. Some put on dazzling light shows to distract predators. Some use boldly colored bodies to slink unseen through the water. And the most successful creatures grow huge or live long. With these special features, deep sea creatures have no need to fear the dark.

Name: ______________________ Date: ______________

Directions: Read "Deep Sea Creatures." Then, answer the questions.

1. Which sentence from the text best describes the main idea?
   - (A) Living things in the deep sea have adapted to a cold, harsh life.
   - (B) Camouflage helps creatures hide from predators.
   - (C) Many deep sea fish have huge eyes.
   - (D) Scientists do not know why animals can grow so big and so old here.

2. What is the topic of the third paragraph?
   - (A) deep sea predators
   - (B) anglerfish are red or pink
   - (C) bioluminescence
   - (D) deep sea camouflage

3. Which adjective does the author use to describe the eyes of a barreleye fish?
   - (A) jar-shaped
   - (B) glowing
   - (C) transparent
   - (D) dazzling

4. Which word is **not** a compound word?
   - (A) oarfish
   - (B) anglerfish
   - (C) vampire
   - (D) lifespans

5. Write a description from the text about each deep sea creature.

Deep Sea Creature	**Description**
vampire squid	
barreleye fish	
anglerfish	
giant oarfish	

Unit 10
WEEK 1
DAY
5

Name: ______________________ Date: ______________

Directions: Reread "Deep Sea Creatures." Then, respond to the prompt.

Imagine you discover a new deep sea creature. Describe what it looks like. Describe interesting things it does to survive. Draw a picture of this new sea creature to go with your writing.

Name: ______________________________ Date: ________________

Directions: Read the text, and answer the questions.

As You Read

Put a ? next to anything that is confusing or that makes you wonder something.

Chimaera Log: Day 1

I've done it! My dream has been realized. I've fused my DNA with that of a chimaera fish. I will become the first deep sea human! I wonder what it will be like to sense electricity. I'll need to hunt prey by finding their electric fields. Will I enjoy the taste of sea urchin?

It's only been hours since the fusion, and already my skin feels a bit rough. It's uncomfortable to move my hands when they're out of water. I'll address this change by increasing the humidity in my lab.

I've built a waterproof device to help me record my experiences. It's like a typewriter with no paper. If I become lost at sea, my research will be saved.

1. What is this text about?
   - (A) a human who has made themselves part fish
   - (B) a human who is SCUBA diving in the deep sea
   - (C) a human who is studying sharks
   - (D) a fish who wants to be a human

2. What is the prefix in the word *uncomfortable*?
   - (A) fort
   - (B) comfort
   - (C) *-able*
   - (D) *un-*

3. What is one thing the narrator wonders about?
   - (A) if he will enjoy eating sea urchins
   - (B) if he will get seasick
   - (C) if he will forget his human life
   - (D) if his computer will work underwater

4. A *log* is a text that is similar to a ______.
   - (A) story
   - (B) poem
   - (C) journal
   - (D) textbook

Name: ______________________ Date: ______________

Directions: Read the text, and answer the questions.

As You Read

Underline words or phrases that describe the narrator.

Chimaera Log: Day 32

My gill slits have opened. I've been breathing cold salt water through them. It's surprisingly refreshing. I'm glad I built such a spacious aquarium. My fins are growing in, and they need plenty of room to stretch. I've also noticed something else. I feel lightheaded after a few minutes out of water. My lungs must be much smaller now. Soon, they'll vanish.

Lately, I've been spending most of my time blindfolded. Light is so painful! Even moonlight gives me a headache. I thought about making myself some goggles, but I'd need new ones every day. My eyes are growing bigger and bigger. They're also moving to the sides of my head. I can't see my nose anymore.

1. What is the setting?
   - (A) the beach
   - (B) an aquarium tank
   - (C) an island
   - (D) the deep sea

2. Which word is an example of an adverb?
   - (A) surprisingly
   - (B) smaller
   - (C) headache
   - (D) vanish

3. Why has the narrator been spending time blindfolded?
   - (A) He can breathe better that way.
   - (B) He wants to see in the dark.
   - (C) He is now very sensitive to light.
   - (D) He is letting his eyes heal.

4. What is a synonym for *vanish*?
   - (A) arrive
   - (B) reappear
   - (C) disappear
   - (D) improve

Name: ______________________ Date: ______________

Directions: Read the text, and answer the questions.

As You Read

Put a ? next to anything that is confusing or that makes you wonder something. Write your questions in the margins.

Chimaera Log: Day 108

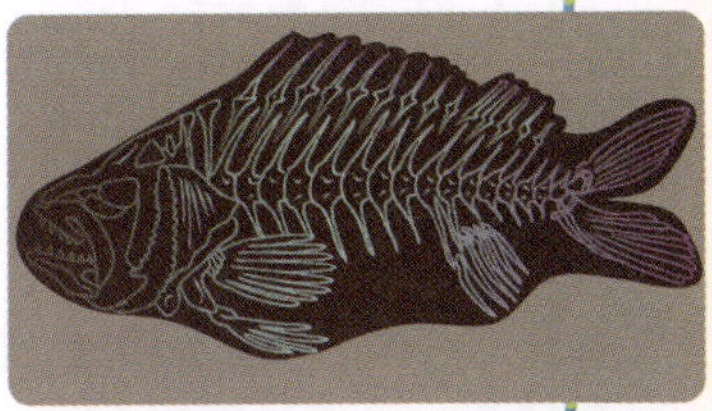

I don't have bones anymore. At first, I didn't notice. It happened so slowly. My bones softened a little more each day. Now, they've been replaced with cartilage. My ribs and the tip of my nose are made from the same stuff. The cartilage will bend under water pressure instead of breaking.

My body has grown accustomed to more and more water pressure. I've been increasing the pressure in my tank every day. In just a few weeks, I should be ready to handle the real ocean. I prepared a submarine to send my tank to the deep.

I get a strange tingle near my nose when living things pass by me. Could this be electroreception?

1. What does the narrator plan to do in a few weeks?
   - (A) go into the ocean
   - (B) get out of the water
   - (C) catch some fish
   - (D) end his experiment

2. What does the prefix *sub–* mean, such as in the word *submarine*?
   - (A) electric
   - (B) boat
   - (C) soft
   - (D) under

3. How is cartilage different from bone?

____

4. Write a prediction for what you think will happen next.

____

____

Name: ______________________ Date: ______________

As You Read

Underline words or phrases that describe the narrator's looks or feelings.

Chimaera Log: Day 1,193

I've done it! I have become a deep sea creature. My eyes are made to catch the faintest flash of light. My nose senses the electric fields of crabs and snails. This strange new feeling is fuzzy at first. It's like television static. Then, as I get closer, the buzz gets sharper. I close in and grind through their shells with my teeth. The electric field goes quiet once the prey stops moving. Then, it's all mine. And oh, the flavor! I preferred shrimp in my human days, but squid is my new favorite.

It's thrilling to hunt prey. I wish a human could hear me explain how it feels to chase electricity. I know things that scientists all over the world want to know. I'm the first human to gain the power of electroreception. I want to tell everyone what this sense is like. But I'm afraid I'll never speak to a human being again. My webbed fingers cannot grasp the tools I used to dive down here. I can't operate a screwdriver, let alone a submarine. If I swim to the surface, the pressure change will crush me. How did I not plan for this?

Deep sea researchers are my only hope of returning to the human world. I dream of seeing a submarine's bright headlight. Sometimes, I think it would be better to forget the human part of me. Feelings like hope and loneliness don't help me hunt. It's useless to sit around waiting to be rescued. It's not all bad, anyway. The seafloor is a beautiful place. There are gorgeous light shows and delicious meals. Plus, hunting leaves me with hardly any time to dwell on the past. So, as time goes on, I'll keep forgetting my human worries. The ocean is the only place for a chimaera-human hybrid like me.

Name: ______________________ Date: ______________

Directions: Read "Chimaera Log: Day 1,193." Then, answer the questions.

1. What problem does the narrator have?

- (A) He cannot handle the pressure.
- (B) He cannot find food.
- (C) He cannot use his fingers.
- (D) He has forgotten how to swim.

2. What is one thing the narrator realizes?

- (A) He should have planned better.
- (B) He must return to the surface.
- (C) He should not be a scientist.
- (D) The deep sea is not that interesting.

3. Which adjective does the narrator use to describe the light shows?

- (A) strange
- (B) thrilling
- (C) delicious
- (D) gorgeous

4. Which word has five syllables?

- (A) researchers
- (B) television
- (C) electricity
- (D) forgetting

5. Describe the narrator at beginning, middle, and end of the story.

Narrator at the Beginning	Narrator in the Middle	Narrator at the End

Name: ______________________ Date: ______________

Directions: Reread "Chimaera Log: Day 1,193." Then, respond to the prompt.

It is now day 2,055. You are the narrator. Write a new log entry. Describe some of your experiences and how you are feeling.

Chimaera Log: Day 2,055

____

____

____

____

____

____

____

____

____

____

____

____

Name: ______________________________ Date: ________________

Anglerfish Love Sonnet

The twinkle of your lure alights your face
So I may gaze into your eyes of pearl
And marvel at the gaping, spiky space
Between your velvet lips, my only girl.

Your swaying lantern shines across the deep
To drag crustaceans in to meet their doom.
And though I have no shell, I wake from sleep
Attracted to your glow amidst the gloom.

Please don't take my advance as a surprise
When I bite you to choose you as my mate.

My body is a fraction of your size.
I'll latch on tight, so you won't feel my weight.

Come close, my love, our union's overdue.
I've always dreamed of being part of you.

Name: ______________________________ Date: ______________

Directions: Read "Anglerfish Love Sonnet." Then, answer the questions.

1. What is the tone of this text?
   - (A) serious
   - (B) romantic
   - (C) mysterious
   - (D) sad

2. Who is the narrator of this poem?
   - (A) a large, female anglerfish
   - (B) a deep sea fisherman
   - (C) a small, male anglerfish
   - (D) a small, male squid

3. What does the author compare the anglerfish's light to?
   - (A) a lantern
   - (B) a flashlight
   - (C) a candle
   - (D) headlights

4. How many stanzas does this poem have?
   - (A) two
   - (B) three
   - (C) four
   - (D) five

5. What line from the poem do you like the best? Why?

____

____

____

____

____

Name: ______________________________ Date: ________________

Directions: Closely read these texts. Then, study the poem on page 185. Look for words or phrases related to deep sea creatures. Write them in the chart.

Close-Reading Texts

Deep Sea Creatures	Chimaera Log: Day 1,193
Living things in the deep sea have adapted to a cold, harsh life. Some put on dazzling light shows to distract predators. Some use boldly colored bodies to slink unseen through the water. And the most successful creatures grow huge or live long. With these special features, deep sea creatures have no need to fear the dark.	I've done it! I have become a deep sea creature. My eyes are made to catch the faintest flash of light. My nose senses the electric fields of crabs and snails. This strange new feeling is fuzzy at first. It's like television static. Then, as I get closer, the buzz gets sharper. I close in and grind through their shells with my teeth. The electric field goes quiet once the prey stops moving. Then, it's all mine. And oh, the flavor! I preferred shrimp in my human days, but squid is my new favorite.

Text	Words or Phrases about Deep Sea Creatures
Deep Sea Creatures	
Chimaera Log: Day 1,193	
Anglerfish Love Sonnet	

Name: ______________________ Date: ______________

Directions: Closely read these texts. Then, compare and contrast the two texts. Think about their purposes, tones, and language. Think about their genres and structures.

Close-Reading Texts

Deep Sea Creatures	Anglerfish Love Sonnet
Camouflage helps creatures hide from predators. It can also help them sneak up on prey. A few colors work well for deep sea camouflage. Many kinds of jellyfish and squid are almost fully transparent. Predators can look right through them. Anglerfish can be black to blend in with the darkness. Other kinds of anglerfish are red or pink. In the deep sea, the color red is invisible. This is because red light does not reach these depths. Transparent animals often have red organs. The red color hides the only visible part of their bodies.	The twinkle of your lure alights your face So I may gaze into your eyes of pearl And marvel at the gaping, spiky space Between your velvet lips, my only girl. Your swaying lantern shines across the deep To drag crustaceans in to meet their doom. And though I have no shell, I wake from sleep Attracted to your glow amidst the gloom.

Deep Sea Creatures	Both	Anglerfish Love Sonnet

Name: ______________________________ **Date:** ______________

Directions: Think about the texts from this unit. Then, respond to the prompt.

Write an opinion paragraph about which deep sea creature you think is the best. Use evidence from the texts to support your opinion.

____

____

____

____

____

____

____

____

____

____

____

____

____

Name: ______________________ Date: ______________

Directions: Write a poem about a deep sea creature. It can rhyme or not. It can be an acrostic poem, a sonnet, or something different. Try to use at least one simile or metaphor in your poem.

Name: ______________________________ Date: ______________

Directions: Read the text, and answer the questions.

As You Read

Write a ∞ wherever you make connections.
Share your connections with a friend or adult.

Two Ways to Be Happy

All people want to feel happy. But what kind of happiness do people want to feel? That depends on their culture. Jeanne Tsai, Ph.D., studies this. She studies a type of science called *psychology*. She found that feeling happy means different things to different groups of people. For example, Chinese people think it is best to be calm. They show that they are happy with closed, peaceful smiles. American people like to be excited. They show that they are happy with open, toothy grins.

1. What are the two different ways to be happy mentioned in the text?
   - (A) to be calm or to be excited
   - (B) to smile or to laugh
   - (C) to be excited or to smile
   - (D) to be calm or to laugh

2. Which has the same root word as *excited*?
   - (A) cited
   - (B) exit
   - (C) excitement
   - (D) excellent

3. The word *psychology* most likely means ______.
   - (A) the study of Chinese and American people
   - (B) the study of different types of smiles
   - (C) the study of the mind, emotions, and behavior
   - (D) the study of what makes people feel excited

4. What is another way to say *toothy grin*?
   - (A) big smile
   - (B) peaceful smile
   - (C) laughter
   - (D) happiness

Name: ______________________ Date: ______________

Directions: Read the text, and answer the questions.

As You Read

Write a ∞ wherever you make connections.
Share your connections with a friend or adult.

Dealing with Strong Feelings

Strong emotions are difficult to handle. When people feel strong feelings, they might think that they can't control what they say or do. But all people can control their emotions. It's as easy as breathing. Breathing controls the heart rate, or the speed of a heartbeat. When strong emotions take over, the heart rate increases. Less blood flows to the brain, and it becomes hard to make good decisions. Taking slow, deep breaths helps slow the heart rate back to normal. This helps blood flow return to the brain.

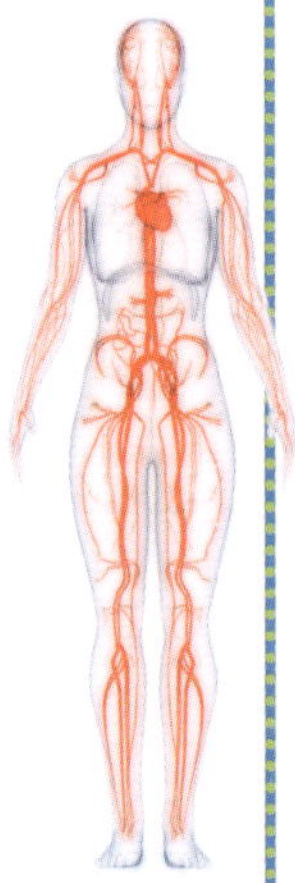

1. What cause does the author give for heart rate increase?
   - (A) controlling your emotions
   - (B) taking slow, deep breaths
   - (C) blood flow returning to the brain
   - (D) strong emotions taking over

2. What can be an effect of less blood flowing to the brain?
   - (A) breathing slowly
   - (B) faster blood low
   - (C) difficulty making good decisions
   - (D) an increase in the heart rate

3. Which sentence shows the author's opinion?
   - (A) Taking slow, deep breaths helps slow the heart rate back to normal.
   - (B) Strong emotions are difficult to handle.
   - (C) Breathing controls the heart rate, or the speed of a heartbeat.
   - (D) This helps blood flow return to the brain.

4. Which word has the same vowel sound as *brain*?
   - (A) rate
   - (B) beat
   - (C) back
   - (D) speed

Name: ______________________ Date: ____________

Directions: Read the text, and answer the questions.

As You Read

Write a ∞ wherever you make connections.
Share your connections with a friend or adult.

Think about Your Thoughts

To stay in good mental health, pay attention to your thoughts. Write them in a journal, or say them out loud. Next, decide whether those thoughts are true or false. For example, maybe your thought is, "I don't know enough to pass the test." If the thought is false, correct it by writing or saying, "I studied hard, and I'm prepared to pass the test." If the thought is true, figure out how to solve that problem. Write or say as many solutions as you can think of. This could look like a numbered list:

1. I can try a new studying method.
2. I can ask my classmates and teachers for help.
3. I can be proud of what I learned, even if I don't pass.

1. What is this text about?

- (A) mental health
- (B) types of lists
- (C) how to study
- (D) good friends

2. Which word is spelled correctly?

- (A) journle
- (B) journal
- (C) jurnal
- (D) journall

3. What is the main idea of this text?

____

4. What else could you add to the list in the text?

____

____

Name: ______________________ Date: ____________

As You Read

Write a ∞ wherever you make connections. Write words or phrases in the margins to describe your connections.

All about Anger

Anger is a normal emotion. People feel angry when they think someone is treating them unfairly. But anger can lead to aggression. Yelling and fighting are aggressive actions. Aggression leads to more aggression. When one person starts a fight, the other person will want to fight back. Then, both people are unable to think clearly. That's why it's important to learn how to deal with anger. When people feel calm, they can solve disagreements with kind words.

The first step to dealing with anger is recognizing it. When you feel angry, what does your body feel like? Do you furrow your eyebrows or clench your teeth? Do your muscles feel tight and make you feel like you can't relax? Or maybe you feel so angry that your skin feels warm. When you feel that way, tell yourself, "I'm angry. I need to calm down."

At first, it seems difficult to calm yourself when you're angry. Some methods of calming down may not help right away. So, remember a few calming skills and figure out what works best for you. Start by taking a few slow, deep breaths. Pay attention to how the air fills up your belly first and then your chest. If you're having a hard time breathing, or if you still don't feel calm, walk away. If you can, go to another room or a small space where you can be alone. Use that space to express your feelings safely. Stuffed toys and pillows are helpful tools for releasing anger. You may feel like yelling, hitting, or throwing things. It's harmful to do that to a person, but pillows don't mind one bit. Other calm activities include drawing, listening to music, and playing with toys or games.

When dealing with an angry person, the best thing to do is stay calm. If they say hurtful things, try not to take it personally. That person might not really be mad at you. They could be having a bad day, and that stress made them say things they don't mean. Instead of arguing back, tell them that you notice their feelings. You might say, "I see that you're feeling upset. Would you like to talk about it? Or would you rather be alone?" If that person does not respond, leave them alone. They will calm down when they're ready.

Name: ______________________________ Date: ______________

Directions: Read "All about Anger." Then, answer the questions.

1. What is one thing the author suggests doing if you are angry?

- (A) breathe quickly
- (B) yell at someone
- (C) listen to music
- (D) drink water

2. Which statement shows a personal connection to the text?

- (A) I am always happy when I play outside.
- (B) I like to listen to music in the car.
- (C) I get nervous about flying.
- (D) I clench my fists when I get angry.

3. What is the root word in *disagreements*?

- (A) disagree
- (B) agreements
- (C) agree
- (D) dis

4. Which topic is **not** covered in the text?

- (A) things people argue about
- (B) ways to calm down
- (C) dealing with angry people
- (D) signs you are angry

5. Write three tips for how to calm down.

Tips to Calm Down

Name: ______________________________ Date: ______________

Directions: Reread "All about Anger." Then, respond to the prompt.

How can you use what you learned from the text in your own life? Write details to explain what you can and will do.

____

____

____

____

____

____

____

____

____

____

____

____

____

Name: ______________________________ Date: ________________

Directions: Read the text, and answer the questions.

As You Read

Write a ∞ wherever you make connections. Write a few words in the margins to describe the connections.

Four Square Friends

Nearly all of Mr. Nides's class liked to play four square. They always played fair, no matter how much they each wanted to win. But one day, Adaly shocked the whole class. One Thursday at recess, Adaly bounced her yellow ball into her classmate Niko's square. Niko lunged for the ball, but it bounced just out of his reach. Adaly did a little victory dance. Niko skidded to the ground. He stood up, brushed himself off, and said, "I'll get you in the next round!"

1. What is the setting?
   - (A) a classroom
   - (B) a library
   - (C) a school playground
   - (D) a soccer field

2. Why does Adaly do a victory dance?
   - (A) She is happy she won.
   - (B) She is happy it is recess.
   - (C) She is excited for school.
   - (D) She is excited for lunch.

3. What genre of text is this?
   - (A) realistic fiction
   - (B) nonfiction
   - (C) fantasy
   - (D) historical fiction

4. Who would likely relate the most to this text?
   - (A) a professional swimmer
   - (B) a high school science teacher
   - (C) a student in elementary school
   - (D) a librarian

Name: ______________________________ Date: ______________

Directions: Read the text, and answer the questions.

As You Read

Write a ∞ wherever you make connections. Write a few words in the margins to describe the connections.

A Close Call

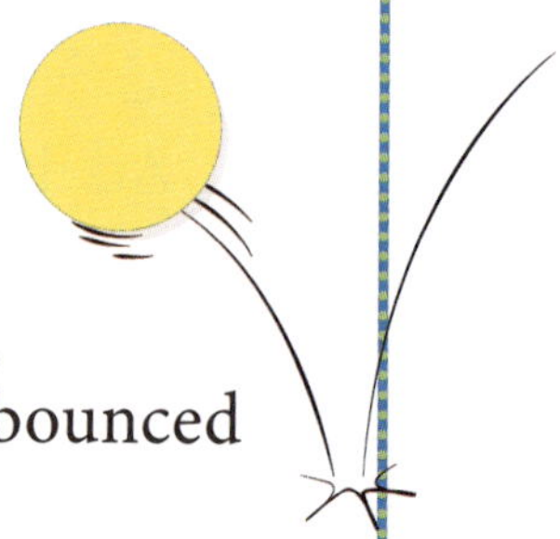

Adaly felt determined to beat Niko in each round they played. She waited patiently. She aimed the ball at the edges of her opponents' squares. Each time, her opponents missed. She struck out one, two, and then three classmates. Finally, Niko was back in the game. When the ball headed toward her, Adaly aimed her fist straight for Niko's square. Yellow rubber bounced against white paint, right at the edge of the court.

"Foul ball, Adaly," said Niko. "Nice try, but that trick won't work every time."

Adaly's friend Lauren went to take her place on the court, but Adaly wouldn't budge. Her feet stood still inside her square, and her fists clenched stiff at her sides.

"The ball bounced inside the court, dummies!" Adaly shouted.

1. How many people does Adaly get out in a row?
   - (A) two
   - (B) three
   - (C) four
   - (D) five

2. Why does Adaly get out in the game?
   - (A) The ball landed outside the court.
   - (B) The ball hit her leg.
   - (C) The ball bounced too many times.
   - (D) The ball bounced on the line.

3. Which word has the same root word as *determined*?
   - (A) determination
   - (B) mining
   - (C) terminate
   - (D) detention

4. Which suffix could replace *–ed* in *bounced* to make a new word?
   - (A) *–ion*
   - (B) *–ing*
   - (C) *–ly*
   - (D) *–ish*

Name: ______________________ Date: ____________

Directions: Read the text, and answer the questions.

As You Read

Write a ∞ wherever you make connections. Write a few words in the margins to describe the connections.

Foul Play

"You need to calm down," Lauren shouted back. "Everyone agreed that if the ball hits the paint, you're out. We're not dummies. You're being a sore loser."

Niko saw that Adaly's face was clenched in fury. Her body was as tense as a tea kettle ready to boil.

"Lauren, you should probably leave her alone," Niko warned. He put his hand on Lauren's shoulder, but she shrugged away from him.

"Dude, she's acting like a huge baby," Lauren replied.

She turned back to Adaly and yelled, "You never act like this. What's wrong with you today?" Lauren reached out to touch her friend's shoulder. Adaly shrank back in fear all of a sudden.

"Get away from me!" Adaly yelled. She pushed Lauren away from her. But she didn't mean to push her so hard.

1. Adaly says, *Get away from me!* to Lauren. Why does this sentence end with an exclamation point?

- (A) Adaly is far from Lauren.
- (B) Adaly is excited.
- (C) Adaly is angry.
- (D) Adaly is frightened.

2. Which phrase is a simile?

- (A) "a sore loser"
- (B) "shrank back in fear"
- (C) "clenched in fury"
- (D) "as tense as a tea kettle ready to boil"

3. Why does Niko tell Lauren she should leave Adaly alone?

____

____

Name: ______________________ Date: ______________

As You Read

Write a ∞ wherever you make connections.

Root of the Problem

Lauren stumbled backward. The ball was behind her, and she tripped right over it. Her own friend had pushed her! She had no idea why. Her first reaction was to get up and push back, but she didn't.

Adaly felt ashamed. She couldn't bring herself to look at anyone. She crouched to the floor and hugged her knees.

Something must be wrong with Adaly, Lauren thought.

"Everyone, let's go play on another court, okay?" Lauren offered.

Everyone walked away, and Adaly was left alone. She studied a line of ants marching across the ground. After a few minutes, Adaly relaxed. Her spine unfurled like a pill bug's, and she sat cross-legged on the court.

Lauren felt like it was safe to return to her friend. She crouched on the ground next to Adaly and asked, "Hey, want to talk about it?"

Adaly felt a sob squeeze her throat. "I'm sorry for pushing you, I'm—I just—I—" she croaked, but her voice faded.

Lauren said, "It's okay. I'll wait until you're ready to talk."

Adaly nodded, wiped her face, and began. "I just wanted to be the best at something for once. Everything's been going wrong lately. I failed my multiplication quiz again."

"Oh man, I know," Lauren agreed. "I got stuck on sixes for a few weeks. I can show you the video later. Do you want to study multiplication with me after school?" she asked.

Adaly blinked at Lauren through her tears. "I'd really appreciate that," she said. "It's so hard to study at my house. My family gets pretty loud, and I don't have any headphones."

Lauren said, "You can borrow mine whenever you visit."

"Yeah, I would like that. And I really am sorry. Next time I feel that angry, I'll calm down before I lash out," said Adaly.

"I forgive you. Next time you feel that angry, I won't bother you so much," Lauren said. She rubbed her friend's shoulder. Adaly leaned her head on her friend's arm. When the bell rang, they walked back to class, elbow in elbow.

Name: ______________________________ Date: ______________

Directions: Read "Root of the Problem." Then, answer the questions.

1. Why does Lauren ask the others to move to another court?

(A) She thinks the other court was better.
(B) She wants to give Adaly some time alone.
(C) She does not want to be friends with Adaly.
(D) She wants to play a different game.

2. Which word best describes the main characters at the end?

(A) friends
(B) enemies
(C) strangers
(D) sisters

3. What is a synonym for *ashamed*?

(A) scared
(B) mad
(C) confused
(D) embarrassed

4. *Her spine unfurled like a pill bug's* is an example of ______.

(A) a metaphor
(B) a simile
(C) hyperbole
(D) alliteration

5. Write details about the story elements of the text.

Root of the Problem	
Characters	**Setting**
Conflict	**Resolution**

Name: ______________________________ Date: ______________

Directions: Reread "Root of the Problem." Then, respond to the prompt.

How might the story have been different if Lauren and the others did not leave Adaly alone for a while? Explain your ideas.

____

____

____

____

____

____

____

____

____

____

____

____

____

Name: ______________________________ Date: ______________

The Last Piece of Chicken

Name: ______________________ Date: ____________

Directions: Read "The Last Piece of Chicken." Then, answer the questions.

1. What is the conflict in this comic story?
   - (A) A brother and sister both want the last piece of chicken.
   - (B) A brother and sister both want a new cat.
   - (C) A brother and sister want different sauce on the chicken.
   - (D) A brother and sister fight over the last seat at the table.

2. What happens after the drumstick lands on the carpet?
   - (A) The brother eats the chicken.
   - (B) The siblings blame each other.
   - (C) The siblings both grab the chicken
   - (D) The cat picks up the chicken in its mouth.

3. Which is **not** an example of onomatopoeia?
   - (A) Clash!
   - (B) Clang!
   - (C) Whoosh!
   - (D) It's mine!

4. Who gets the drumstick in the end?
   - (A) the mouse
   - (B) the cat
   - (C) the brother
   - (D) the sister

5. Write one or two sentences that summarize the events of the comic.

____

____

____

____

____

Name: ____________________ Date: ____________

Directions: Closely read these texts. Look for words or phrases that show a person is angry. Write them in the chart. Use three of the words or phrases to write your own sentences.

Close-Reading Texts

Foul Play	All about Anger
Niko saw that Adaly's face was clenched in fury. Her body was as tense as a tea kettle ready to boil. Lauren reached out to touch her friend's shoulder. Adaly shrank back in fear all of a sudden. "Get away from me!" Adaly yelled. She pushed Lauren away from her.	The first step to dealing with anger is recognizing it. When you feel angry, what does your body feel like? Do you furrow your eyebrows or clench your teeth? Do your muscles feel tight and make you feel like you can't relax? Or maybe you feel so angry that your skin feels warm.

Text	Signs of Anger
Foul Play	
All about Anger	

1. ________________________________

2. ________________________________

3. ________________________________

Name: ______________________ Date: ______________

Directions: Closely read these texts. Study the comic on page 203. Then answer the questions on the chart.

Close-Reading Texts

Excerpt 1 from "Root of the Problem"	Excerpt 2 from "Root of the Problem"
Lauren stumbled backward. The ball was behind her, and she tripped right over it. Her own friend had pushed her! She had no idea why. Her first reaction was to get up and push back, but she didn't. Adaly felt ashamed. She couldn't bring herself to look at anyone. She crouched to the floor and hugged her knees.	"And I really am sorry. Next time I feel that angry, I'll calm down before I lash out," said Adaly. "I forgive you. Next time you feel that angry, I won't bother you so much," Lauren said. She rubbed her friend's shoulder. Adaly leaned her head on her friend's arm. When the bell rang, they walked back to class, elbow in elbow.

Question	Root of the Problem	The Last Piece of Chicken
What is the setting?		
What is the conflict?		
What happens at the end?		

Name: ______________________________ Date: ______________

Directions: Think about the texts from this unit. Then, respond to the prompt.

Write a letter to one of the characters in the text "Root of the Problem." Give them some advice on how to deal with anger. Ask them some questions.

______________________________,

____

____

____

____

____

____

____

____

____

______________________________,

____

Name: ______________________________ Date: ______________

Directions: Create your own comic-style story. Tell the story with pictures. Add some words or captions to help explain what is happening.

Name: ______________________ Date: ______________

Directions: Read the text, and answer the questions.

As You Read

Underline information that is new to you. Put a star next to information you already know.

The Wright Brothers

The airplane is an amazing invention. Two brothers flew an airplane first. Orville and Wilbur Wright were the inventors. The Wright brothers studied flight for many years. They began their work with kites. They learned a lot about how kites fly. They flew an airplane for the first time in 1903.

Wright Brothers' 1903 Flyer

1. Which summary of the text is most accurate?
   - Ⓐ This text is about different kinds of inventions.
   - Ⓑ This text is about different methods of transportation.
   - Ⓒ This text is about space.
   - Ⓓ This text is about how the airplane was invented.

2. Which index entry would direct a reader to this text?
   - Ⓐ Wright, Orville and Wilbur
   - Ⓑ different kinds of airplanes
   - Ⓒ airports
   - Ⓓ the physics of flights

3. Which suffix could replace *–ed* in *learned* to make a new word?
   - Ⓐ *–er*
   - Ⓑ *–ly*
   - Ⓒ *–tion*
   - Ⓓ *–ment*

4. What is an example of an amazing invention in today's world?
   - Ⓐ pencil
   - Ⓑ bread
   - Ⓒ smart watches
   - Ⓓ clothing

Name: ______________________________ Date: ______________

Directions: Read the text, and answer the questions.

As You Read

Underline information that is new to you. Put a star next to information you already know.

Flying across the Atlantic

The Atlantic Ocean is the second largest ocean. Airplanes cross this ocean each day. They are called *transatlantic flights*. Early engineers had to figure out how to cross this ocean. Planes could not travel far enough to cross it. The engines were not strong enough. The first planes could not hold enough fuel, either. Today, long flights across the Atlantic are very common. This is a big change from the past.

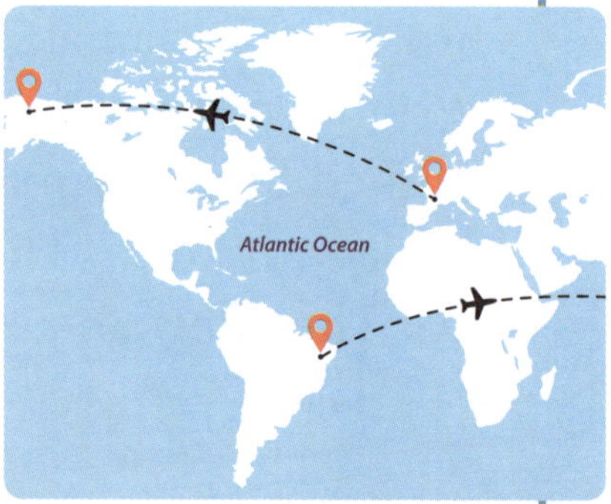

1. Which word tells a reader most about the topic of this text?
   - Ⓐ pilot
   - Ⓑ transatlantic
   - Ⓒ travel
   - Ⓓ water

2. Which suffix could replace *–est* in *largest* to make a new word?
   - Ⓐ *–ion*
   - Ⓑ *–ing*
   - Ⓒ *–ed*
   - Ⓓ *–er*

3. Which definition of the word *cross* is used in this text?
   - Ⓐ angry
   - Ⓑ a figure of two lines perpendicular to each other
   - Ⓒ to go over
   - Ⓓ mixture

4. What does it mean that transatlantic flights *are very common*?
   - Ⓐ They are safe.
   - Ⓑ They happen often.
   - Ⓒ They are organized.
   - Ⓓ They fly in circles.

Name: ______________________ Date: ______________

Directions: Read the text, and answer the questions.

As You Read

Underline information that is new to you. Put a star next to information you already know.

A Plane's Altitude

Altitude refers to the height of a plane in the air from the ground. It is an important part of flying. There are rules for how high or low planes can fly. These rules are for safety. Instruments in the plane let the pilot know about altitude. An *altimeter* is one of the tools in a plane that measures altitude. It is located in the cockpit. This is where the pilot or pilots sit.

instruments in the cockpit of an old plane

1. Which statement uses the first sentence to accurately preview the text?
   - (A) I think this text is about bird's flight.
   - (B) I think this text is about landing and taking off in an airplane.
   - (C) I think this text is about the flight level of airplanes.
   - (D) I think this text is about the altitude of a tall mountain.

2. Which words from the text are synonyms?
   - (A) *instrument* and *tool*
   - (B) *part* and *air*
   - (C) *safety* and *off*
   - (D) *ground* and *low*

3. Why do pilots need to pay attention to altitude?

   ____

   ____

   ____

4. What do you think it would be like to fly a plane?

   ____

   ____

   ____

   ____

Name: ______________________ Date: ______________

As You Read

Underline information you think is important or interesting. Write a few of your thoughts in the margins.

The Life of Amelia Earhart

Amelia Earhart wanted to fly planes from a young age. She was born in 1897 in Kansas. She loved to climb trees. She hunted rats with a rifle. During her childhood, airplanes became more common. She took her first flight in 1920. She was hooked. This ride changed her life.

Earhart took her first flying lesson in 1921. She worked hard to save money. She was a nurse's aide. Then she worked as a social worker. She put all her money into savings. Soon, she had enough to buy her first plane!

Earhart's first plane was bright yellow. She called it *Canary*. Earhart learned a lot about flying in that plane. She flew to an altitude of 14,000 feet (4,267 meters). She set a record. No one else had done that before. Her next record was being the first woman to fly across the Atlantic Ocean. She joined two other pilots. She sat in their plane as a passenger. Together, they made the flight in about 21 hours.

Earhart set her sights on the next record. This time, she wanted to fly the Atlantic alone. She wanted to do a solo flight. Her husband helped her plan the trip. He wanted to help her reach her goal. In 1932, she was ready. She started in Newfoundland, Canada. She was flying to Paris, France. But bad weather forced her to land in Ireland. Still, this was a victory for her. She showed the world that both men and women could safely fly solo across the Atlantic.

Earhart set out to beat another challenge. She wanted to be the first woman to fly around the world. On June 1, 1937, she started her trip. She left from Miami, Florida. She traveled over 20,000 miles (32,186 kilometers). At last, she was reaching the end! It was July 2. The weather was cloudy and wet. She took off from New Guinea. Earhart had a hard time hearing messages on her radio. She reported that she was "running north and south." Then the line was silent. Those were Earhart's last words. She was never seen again. Her plane was not found, either. Experts are still trying to solve this mystery.

Throughout Earhart's life, her bravery was inspiring. She showed the world that strong women can do great things!

Name: ______________________ Date: ____________

Directions: Read "The Life of Amelia Earhart." Then, answer the questions.

1. What is the main reason for reading a biography?

- (A) to learn about history
- (B) to compare the lives of famous people
- (C) to learn about a person's life story
- (D) to learn about a person's family

2. Which statement shows a helpful connection to Amelia Earhart?

- (A) I have been to Miami on a vacation with my family.
- (B) I once took train to my grandmother's house across the country.
- (C) I tried out for the boys' soccer team to prove girls can play soccer just as well.
- (D) My doctor has a nurse and a nurse's aide.

3. What is the most important idea about Amelia Earhart's life?

- (A) She flew better than anyone else.
- (B) She took chances, was brave, and taught people about equality.
- (C) She liked to beat records.
- (D) It is not known if she is dead or alive or where her plane ended up.

4. What is one way in which Amelia Earhart took chances?

- (A) by climbing trees
- (B) by learning to fly a plane
- (C) by learning to fly a plane solo
- (D) all of the above

5. Write three major events in Amelia Earhart's life. Write them in the order they occurred.

Date	Event

Name: ______________________ Date: ____________

Directions: Reread "The Life of Amelia Earhart." Then, respond to the prompt.

Finish writing an opinion about Amelia Earhart. Read the opinion statement. Write facts and details to support the opinion.

Amelia Earhart was brave and courageous. ____________________

Name: ______________________ Date: ____________

Directions: Read the text, and answer the questions.

As You Read

Underline words or phrases that describe the setting.

Vexben Galaxy, 700 Kilometers from Plyzon

"Whoa, Captain, watch out," cried Oosa. A trash bin floated dangerously close to their spaceship. The bin clattered against the ship. More space garbage fluttered past the windows.

"No matter, just press the windshield wiper," said the Captain. Oosa stared at the ship's dashboard. He was still learning to be a pilot, so he took time to find the right button.

Oosa pressed his webbed finger against a blue button, and...*squeak!* A bleak view lay beyond the garbage veil. There was more trash, as far as the eye could see—and it only got worse.

1. What is the setting?

- (A) an airplane
- (B) the deep sea
- (C) outer space
- (D) a garbage pit

2. Who is the main character?

- (A) Oosa
- (B) the captain
- (C) the spaceship
- (D) the button

3. Which word from the text is an onomatopoeia?

- (A) veil
- (B) bleak
- (C) squeak
- (D) wiper

4. What is the meaning of the phrase *as far as the eye could see*?

- (A) a very long distance away
- (B) a very short distance away
- (C) only visible at night
- (D) very bright

Name: ______________________ Date: ______________

Directions: Read the text, and answer the questions.

As You Read

Underline words or phrases that describe the planet Plyzon.

Plyzon, Atmosphere Zone 1

"Hold on, Oosa," the Captain ordered. "We're headed toward the planet Plyzon. The atmosphere is full of far worse junk than that."

Oosa and the Captain buckled their seatbelts. Oosa looked out the window. Clouds of smoke billowed out of the planet below. Each cloud shimmered a different color. Reds, yellows, and greens swirled across its sky.

"I've never been to Plyzon before. We can hardly see, but the air is beautiful," said Oosa.

"Beautiful, but vile," the Captain spat. "The air is nothing more than toxic smog full of dye."

1. Where are the characters in the story headed?
   - (A) a factory
   - (B) Earth
   - (C) the planet Plyzon
   - (D) to their home planet

2. Which statement describes the air on Plyzon?
   - (A) It is colorful, but it is toxic.
   - (B) It looks ugly, but is fresh.
   - (C) It looks clear and smells great.
   - (D) It is gray and toxic.

3. What is a synonym for *beautiful*?
   - (A) pretty
   - (B) ugly
   - (C) smokey
   - (D) colorful

4. What is an antonym for *below*?
   - (A) slow
   - (B) behind
   - (C) underneath
   - (D) above

Name: ______________________________ Date: ______________

Directions: Read the text, and answer the questions.

As You Read

Circle words or phrases that describe characters' actions.

Plyzon, Atmosphere Zone 6

Oosa fumbled over the dashboard. He raised the ship's shield. "Now we'll be safe until landing," he sighed.

Suddenly, the ship swerved to the right to avoid some junk. Oosa's seatbelt tightened on his chest. A wave of ancient, broken electronics floated by. Loose, rusty wires tickled the sides of the spacecraft.

"Prepare for a bumpy ride," the Captain cackled. She yanked the steering disc to and fro. Oosa's stomach began to feel a bit nauseous.

1. What does the word *suddenly* tell readers about the event?
   - (A) It is a surprise.
   - (B) It happens slowly.
   - (C) They plan for it.
   - (D) It is fun for them.

2. What does the phrase *to and fro* mean?
   - (A) in circles
   - (B) back and forth
   - (C) quick then slow
   - (D) very quickly

3. Write one or two sentences that summarize what happens in the text.

____

____

4. Write a prediction about what you think will happen next.

____

____

Name: ______________________ Date: ______________

As You Read

Visualize what is happening in the story. Underline words, phrases, or sentences that are the most helpful for your visualization.

Surface of Plyzon

Oosa was grateful when the Captain slowed the spaceship. Here, the atmosphere's pressure changed. Space junk no longer floated. Instead, it fell. Oosa realized that their spaceship was about to fall, too.

"Here we go!" cried the Captain. The ship took a nosedive toward Plyzon. Oosa was terrified. Flaming trash rained from the sky. He did his best to clear debris from the windshield.

After a moment, the Captain said, "Oosa, we're about to land!"

"Where?" Oosa shrieked. "It's impossible to see anything! The smoke is too thick!"

"Follow that blinking blue trail," the Captain instructed calmly. Oosa looked down and saw neon lights.

Oosa helped swing the ship toward them. Together, they brought the ship lower, and lower still, until it settled on the ground. Dust flew out in all directions. Hot wind scorched the rocks where it landed.

The back of the spaceship opened like a flower. With a *kshh-chkk-whirr*, a ramp unfolded from the ship. Huge orange crates of cargo rolled down the ramp. Each crate was taller than two Earthlings. Finally, the Captain and Oosa stepped out. They looked as small as bugs next to their cargo crates.

A Space Customs agent waited to meet them on the ground. The agent inspected the cargo. They wiggled their tentacles in approval.

"Everything is here," the agent said. "Three hundred thousand units of QualiCool Air Dye."

"QualiCool Hair Dye?" Oosa asked.

"*Air* dye, spelled A-I-R," the agent corrected. "Helps get our skies that naturally rosy pink color. Just like what sunsets on Earth used to be!"

"Oh, I see. We hope you're satisfied with your purchase. Please fill out these electronic forms," Oosa said. He slid the agent a holo-chip. The agent plugged the holo-chip into his wrist to sign the forms.

"It was a pleasure doing business with you," Oosa said.

"A *real* pleasure," said the Captain, rolling her eyes.

Name: ______________________________ Date: ______________

Directions: Read "Surface of Plyzon." Then, answer the questions.

1. Why is it hard for Oosa to see?

- Ⓐ It is dark.
- Ⓑ There is thick smoke.
- Ⓒ His glasses fall off.
- Ⓓ The window is cracked.

2. What is the captain's tone when she says the phrase, "A *real* pleasure"?

- Ⓐ scared
- Ⓑ sarcastic
- Ⓒ confused
- Ⓓ serious

3. What do the captain and Oosa drop off on Plyzon?

- Ⓐ tools
- Ⓑ food
- Ⓒ paint
- Ⓓ air dye

4. What genre of text is this?

- Ⓐ biography
- Ⓑ nonfiction
- Ⓒ science fiction
- Ⓓ historical fiction

5. Summarize four events in the story, and write them in the order they occur.

Event 1	
Event 2	
Event 3	
Event 4	

Name: ______________________________ Date: ______________

Directions: Reread "Surface of Plyzon." Then, respond to the prompt.

Would you like to be a character in this story? Why or why not? Explain your thinking with evidence from the text.

___

___

___

___

___

___

___

___

___

___

___

___

___

Name: ______________________ Date: ______________

Aerobatics Article

FOLSOM FOLLIES FORCED TO FOUL BERRY FIELD

"You can't miss the fun at Folsom Follies' Spectacular Flight! Witness the triplets' acrobatic airplane tricks!" That's what last Sunday's paper said, anyway. The famous Folsoms came to town. But their flight didn't go according to plan.

"It all seemed to be going well. Two of the twins flew three loops in the sky. It was incredible," said Marcus Campbell, a local farmer. "Then, catastrophe struck."

The Folsom brothers tried to perform another stunt. Both brothers jumped out of the cockpit and stood on the plane's wings. The plane was unable to steer itself. It veered to the ground.

"Right then, we all realized there should be three Folsoms," Campbell said.

The third Folsom triplet had never boarded the plane. Mary Folsom's brothers left her behind. Apparently, this was not the first time. Mary's friends describe her as "real quiet, but a darn good pilot." Her mother Aquaria said, "I've sat on her more than a few times. She wouldn't say a word."

Luckily, Terry Folsom saved their blunder. He jumped back into the plane. Then, he made a crash landing in Marcus Campbell's strawberry field. His brother Barry Folsom was flung into the field.

"Half the crop's gone, but I'm more worried about those brothers," Campbell said.

The Quilltown Daily asked the Folsoms for comment. None responded to our request. Mary Folsom is still at large. Terry Folsom is suffering from a fractured jaw. Barry Folsom has been badly burned. Their doctor expects both to recover in a few months.

Name: ______________________________ Date: ________________

Directions: Read "Aerobatics Article." Then, answer the questions.

1. What is the tone of this fictional article?

- (A) serious
- (B) humorous
- (C) sad
- (D) hopeful

2. The title of the article, "Folsom Follies Forced to Foul Berry Field," is an example of what?

- (A) hyperbole
- (B) simile
- (C) metaphor
- (D) alliteration

3. What is a synonym for *catastrophe*?

- (A) surprise
- (B) disaster
- (C) miracle
- (D) collision

4. Where does the plane land?

- (A) a strawberry field
- (B) an airport
- (C) a city street
- (D) a lake

5. People really did this type of thing in the 1920s. It was called *barnstorming*. Would you try it? Why or why not?

____

____

____

____

____

____

____

____

Name: ______________________________ Date: ________________

Directions: Closely read this text. Then, reread the fictional article on page 221. Write a dialogue Amelia Earhart might have with Terry Folsom.

Close-Reading Text

The Life of Amelia Earhart

Earhart's first plane was bright yellow. She called it *Canary*. Earhart learned a lot about flying in that plane. She flew to an altitude of 14,000 feet (4,267 meters). She set a record. No one else had done that before. Her next record was being the first woman to fly across the Atlantic Ocean. She joined two other pilots. She sat in their plane as a passenger. Together, they made the flight in about 21 hours.

Earhart set her sights on the next record. This time, she wanted to fly the Atlantic alone. She wanted to do a solo flight. Her husband helped her plan the trip. He wanted to help her reach her goal. In 1932, she was ready. She started in Newfoundland, Canada. She was flying to Paris, France. But bad weather forced her to land in Ireland.

Name: ______________________ Date: ______________

Directions: Closely read these texts. Then compare and contrast Amelia Earhart with Oosa from the fiction story.

Close-Reading Texts

The Life of Amelia Earhart	Surface of Plyzon
She left from Miami, Florida. She traveled over 20,000 miles (32,186 kilometers). At last, she was reaching the end! It was July 2. The weather was cloudy and wet. She took off from New Guinea. Earhart had a hard time hearing messages on her radio. She reported that she was "running north and south." Then the line was silent. Those were Earhart's last words. She was never seen again. Her plane was not found, either. Experts are still trying to solve this mystery.	The ship took a nosedive toward Plyzon. Oosa was terrified. Flaming trash rained from the sky. He did his best to clear debris from the windshield. After a moment, the Captain said, "Oosa, we're about to land!" "Where?" Oosa shrieked. "It's impossible to see anything! The smoke is too thick!" "Follow that blinking blue trail," the Captain instructed calmly. Oosa looked down and saw neon lights.

Amelia Earhart	Oosa

Both

Name: ______________________________ Date: ________________

Directions: Think about the texts from this unit. Then, respond to the prompt.

Write an opinion about which of the following you would rather be:

- a real pilot, like Amelia Earhart
- a pilot of a spaceship, like Oosa
- an aerobatic pilot, like the Folsom triplets

Support your opinion with reasons.

____

____

____

____

____

____

____

____

____

____

____

____

Name: ______________________ Date: ______________

Directions: You are a reporter. Write an article describing Amelia Earhart's last flight. Include some comments from people who knew her. Draw a picture.

Standards Correlations

Shell Education is committed to producing educational materials that are research and standards based. To support this effort, this resource is correlated to the academic standards of all 50 states, the District of Columbia, the Department of Defense Dependent Schools, and the Canadian provinces. A correlation is also provided for key professional educational organizations.

To print a customized correlation report for your state, visit our website at **www.tcmpub.com/administrators/correlations** and follow the online directions. If you require assistance in printing correlation reports, please contact the Customer Service Department at 1-800-858-7339.

Standards Overview

The Every Student Succeeds Act (ESSA) mandates that all states adopt challenging academic standards that help students meet the goal of college and career readiness. While many states already adopted academic standards prior to ESSA, the act continues to hold states accountable for detailed and comprehensive standards. Standardware is also used to develop standardized tests to evaluate students' academic progress. State standards are used in the development of our resources, so educators can be assured they meet state academic requirements.

College and Career Readiness

Today's college and career readiness (CCR) standards offer guidelines for preparing K–12 students with the knowledge and skills that are necessary to succeed in postsecondary job training and education. CCR standards include the Common Core State Standards as well as other state-adopted standards such as the Texas Essential Knowledge and Skills. The standards found on page 228 describe the content presented throughout the lessons.

TESOL and WIDA Standards

English language development standards are integrated within each lesson to enable English learners to work toward proficiency in English while learning content–developing the skills and confidence in listening, speaking, reading, and writing. The standards found in the digital resources describe the language objectives presented throughout the lessons

Standards Correlations *(cont.)*

180 Days of Reading for Third Grade, 2nd Edition, offers a full page of daily reading comprehension and word analysis practice activities for each day of the school year.

Every third grade unit provides questions and activities tied to a wide variety of language arts standards, providing students opportunities for regular practice in reading comprehension, word recognition, and writing. The focus of the first two weeks in each unit alternates between nonfiction and fiction standards, with the third week focusing on both, as students read nontraditional texts and complete paired-text activities.

Reading Comprehension
Read and comprehend complex literary and informational texts independently and proficiently.
Read closely to determine what the text says explicitly. Ask and answer questions about the text and make logical inferences.
Determine central ideas or themes of a text and analyze their development; summarize the key supporting details and ideas.
Analyze how and why individuals, events, or ideas develop and interact over the course of a text.
Recognize and analyze genre-specific characteristics, structures, and purposes within and across diverse texts.
Use metacognitive skills to both develop and deepen comprehension of texts.
Analyze how two or more texts address similar themes or topics to build knowledge or to compare the approaches the authors take.
Assess how point of view or purpose shapes the content and style of texts.
Reading Foundational Skills
Know and apply grade-level phonics and word analysis skills in decoding words.
Language and Vocabulary Acquisition
Determine or clarify the meaning of unknown and multiple-meaning words and phrases by using context clues, analyzing meaningful word parts, and consulting general and specialized reference materials, as appropriate.
Demonstrate understanding of figurative language, word relationships, and nuances in word meanings.
Writing
Produce clear and coherent writing in which the development, organization, and style are appropriate to task, purpose, genre, and audience.
Respond to and draw evidence from literary or informational texts to show analysis, reflection, and research.

Writing Rubric

Score students' written responses using this rubric. Display the rubric for students to reference as they write. A student version of this rubric is provided in the digital resources.

Points	Criteria
4	• Uses an appropriate organizational sequence to produce very clear and coherent writing. • Uses descriptive language that develops or clarifies ideas. • Engages the reader. • Uses a style very appropriate to task, purpose, and audience.
3	• Uses an organizational sequence to produce clear and coherent writing. • Uses descriptive language that develops or clarifies ideas. • Engages the reader. • Uses a style appropriate to task, purpose, and audience.
2	• Uses an organizational sequence to produce somewhat clear and coherent writing. • Uses some descriptive language that develops or clarifies ideas. • Engages the reader in some way. • Uses a style somewhat appropriate to task, purpose, and audience.
1	• Does not use an organized sequence; the writing is not clear or coherent. • Uses little descriptive language to develop or clarify ideas. • Does not engage the reader. • Does not use a style appropriate to task, purpose, or audience.
0	• Offers no writing or does not respond to the assignment presented.

References Cited

Gough, Philip B., and William E. Tunmer. 1986. "Decoding, Reading, and Reading Disability." *Remedial and Special Education* 7 (1): 6–10.

Marzano, Robert. 2010. "When Practice Makes Perfect...Sense." *Educational Leadership* 68 (3): 81–83.

National Reading Panel. 2000. *Report of the National Reading Panel: Teaching Children to Read. Report of the Subgroups*. Washington, D.C.: U.S. Department of Health and Human Services, National Institutes of Health.

Scarborough, Hollis S. 2001. "Connecting Early Language and Literacy to Later Reading (Dis)abilities: Evidence, Theory, and Practice." In *Handbook of Early Literacy Research*, edited by Susan B. Neuman and David K. Dickinson, 97–110. New York: Guilford.

Soalt, Jennifer. 2005. "Bringing Together Fictional and Informational Texts to Improve Comprehension." *The Reading Teacher* 58 (7): 680–683.

Answer Key

Unit 1

Week 1

Day 1 (page 11)

1. D
2. A
3. D
4. B

Day 2 (page 12)

1. C
2. B
3. C
4. A

Day 3 (page 13)

1. A
2. A
3. A regulator is a tool climbers carry that gives them oxygen.
4. Responses should share which piece of climbing gear they think is most important and why.

Day 4 (page 15)

1. C
2. C
3. A
4. C
5. Answers should include three details that tell why Mt. Everest is an amazing place and the people who climb it are brave and strong.

Day 5 (page 16)

Written opinions should include reasons why they would or would not want to climb Mt. Everest.

Week 2

Day 1 (page 17)

1. B
2. A
3. D
4. C

Day 2 (page 18)

1. C
2. A
3. B
4. D

Day 3 (page 19)

1. D
2. B
3. Pictures should show a volcano erupting.

Day 4 (page 21)

1. A
2. B
3. C
4. A
5. Answers should compare how the Crust feels and looks at the beginning and end of the story. For example, *Crust wants everything to be equal at the beginning. Crust appreciates change at the end.*

Day 5 (page 22)

Journal entries should be written from the point of view of the Core and explain what is happening, how they feel, and what they think will happen next.

Week 3

Day 1 (page 24)

1. A
2. D
3. B
4. D
5. Answers should describe what information on the flyer they think would be most important to them and why.

Day 2 (page 25)

Answers should include dialogues between mountain climbers and animals from the story, such as goats.

Day 3 (page 26)

Example

Climbing Mt. Everest	**Adventure Ad**
This text is mostly about the camps at Mt. Everest.	This text is about things to do at a campground near Mt. Goldfish.
Both	
They are both about camps. They both talk about mountains.	

Day 4 (page 27)

Written opinions should describe whether they think landforms make Earth a better place and why.

Day 5 (page 28)

Flyers should be about Mount Everest to persuade people to visit.

Unit 2

Week 1

Day 1 (page 29)

1. C
2. B
3. C
4. A

Day 2 (page 30)

1. B
2. B
3. D
4. D

Day 3 (page 31)

1. A
2. B
3. The main idea is that beach pollution is harmful to animals, but people can help.
4. Answers should explain why pollution is harmful to ocean animals.

Day 4 (page 33)

1. C
2. B
3. C
4. C
5. Answers should include three beach safety tips from the text, such as not going in the water when there's a red flag, only swimming if there's a lifeguard, and being cautious if there is a yellow flag.

Day 5 (page 34)

Answers should summarize the flag colors at the beach and include pictures to support text.

Week 2

Day 1 (page 35)

1. A
2. A
3. B
4. B

Day 2 (page 36)

1. D
2. A
3. D
4. D

Answer Key *(cont.)*

Day 3 (page 37)

1. B
2. D
3. A summary of the text is that Marlo and Jada were at the beach, and Jada injured her foot on something.
4. Answers should include which character students relate to most with one reason given.

Day 4 (page 39)

1. D
2. B
3. A
4. D

Example

Characters: Marlo and Jade

Setting: at the beach

Problem: Jada hurt her foot and does not know what happened.

Solution: They went to a lifeguard, and he told them it was a stingray and how to treat it.

Day 5 (page 40)

Book reviews should share students' opinions and why they would or would not recommend the book to someone else.

Week 3

Day 1 (page 42)

1. C
2. A
3. C
4. A
5. Answers should include the information on the job posting that would be most important if the student wanted to apply.

Day 2 (page 43)

Example

Text	Author's Purpose
Being Safe on the Beach	The author wants to explain the flag colors at the beach.
Beach Detectives	The author wants to entertain readers with a story and show the problem the character has.
Summer Job	The author wants to inform people how to apply to be lifeguards.

Day 3 (page 44)

Example

Beach Detectives: fictional story, injury at the beach, get help from a lifeguard

Being Safe on the Beach: informational/nonfiction, explains what lifeguards do

Both: deals with the beach, talks about lifeguards

Day 4 (page 45)

Stories should take place at the beach, have something to do with beach safety, and have a beginning, middle, and end.

Day 5 (page 46)

Posters should have job postings with details about the available job.

Unit 3

Week 1

Day 1 (page 47)

1. B
2. A
3. A
4. A

Day 2 (page 48)

1. A
2. C
3. B
4. A

Day 3 (page 49)

1. D
2. A
3. Aqueducts are structures that carry water from place to place and are often shaped like arches.
4. Answers should include opinions about why students would or would not want to have lived in ancient Rome.

Day 4 (page 51)

1. A
2. D
3. B
4. D
5. Answers should include five events in Julius Caesar's life.

Example: He was born in 100 BCE; He fell in love with and married Cornelia; He joined the army; He became a leader of the Senate; He was killed by a member of the Senate.

Day 5 (page 52)

Responses should share why students think Julius Caesar was or was not a smart leader.

Week 2

Day 1 (page 53)

1. B
2. A
3. A
4. C

Day 2 (page 54)

1. A
2. A
3. B
4. B

Day 3 (page 55)

1. A
2. B
3. The new law is that chariots will not be allowed in the city during the day.
4. Answers should include one question students would ask Tullia in the story.

Day 4 (page 57)

1. D
2. C
3. A
4. A
5. Graphic organizers should include the effects of three causes from the story.

Examples

1. Tullia goes to the market.
2. The town is very quiet during the day.
3. All the people in Rome groaned.

Answer Key (cont.)

Day 5 (page 58)

Answers should explain whether the student would prefer no chariots during the day or at night.

Week 3

Day 1 (page 60)

1. B
2. C
3. D
4. A
5. Written responses should explain if students would like to make the garum recipe or not.

Day 2 (page 61)

Example

Text	Words and Phrases about Ancient Rome
Water in Ancient Rome	very hot, water to stay cool, liked to be clean, good water system, fresh water inside, near clean water
A Roman Morning	crowded cobblestone street, horse hooves, chariot wheels, had to yell to be heard, sound of metal, noisy

Day 3 (page 62)

Examples

Julius Caesar: did not go to school, boy, important in history

Tullia: young girl, liked to weave

Both: lived in ancient Rome, simple home, not rich or poor

Day 4 (page 63)

Diary entries should be written from the point of view of a person who lives in ancient Rome.

Day 5 (page 64)

Written responses should explain how to make a favorite snack or meal.

Unit 4

Week 1

Day 1 (page 65)

1. B
2. D
3. C
4. C

Day 2 (page 66)

1. D
2. C
3. B
4. B

Day 3 (page 67)

1. B
2. A
3. The main idea is that the World Cup is the biggest soccer competition in the world.
4. Answers should explain why students would or would not like to go to a World Cup game.

Day 4 (page 69)

1. C
2. C
3. D
4. B
5. Responses should include four events that happened in David Beckham's career.
   Example
   He played his first professional game; He got a lot of attention from a goal he made; He was transferred to Real Madrid; He played with the Los Angeles Galaxy.

Day 5 (page 70)

Written letters to David Beckham should ask him questions and tell him what students think about him.

Week 2

Day 1 (page 71)

1. C
2. D
3. B
4. C

Day 2 (page 72)

1. A
2. B
3. A
4. D

Day 3 (page 73)

1. A
2. C
3. Answers should describe pictures that would help readers understand the text, such as a young girl looking nervous in class.
4. Answers should explain the connections students have to the text.

Day 4 (page 75)

1. A
2. D
3. C
4. D
5. *Example Summaries*

Beginning—The narrator wants to learn how to be a great athlete.

Middle—The narrator watches a soccer game and takes a math test.

End—The narrator plays in a big game, but misses an important shot.

Day 5 (page 76)

Answers should include students' own versions of how the story ends.

Week 3

Day 1 (page 78)

1. B
2. A
3. C
4. C
5. Written responses should include what information on the flyer students think would be most important to them and what else they would like to know.

Answer Key *(cont.)*

Day 2 (page 79)

Example

Nouns	Verbs
soccer, skills, game, Manchester United	played, worked
forward position, ball, goal	playing, running, passing, practiced
soccer, skills, tricks, field	exercise, practice, learn

Day 3 (page 80)

Example Comparisons

David Beckham: made an important goal, shot when the goalie was out of the goal

Narrator: missed an important goal, shot the ball at the goalie

Both: tried to make a very important goal, play soccer

Day 4 (page 81)

Diary entries should be written from the perspective of the narrator from the story at their first day of soccer camp.

Day 5 (page 82)

Flyers should advertise David Beckham coming to sign autographs.

Unit 5

Week 1

Day 1 (page 83)

1. C
2. B
3. A
4. C

Day 2 (page 84)

1. A
2. C
3. B
4. B

Day 3 (page 85)

1. D
2. C
3. Answers should include at least three of the following: salty, saltier, sweet, bitter, intense
4. Answers should describe what students think are the pros and cons of being a supertaster.

Day 4 (page 87)

1. C
2. B
3. A
4. C
5. Written responses should detail what led to the invention of chewing gum.

Day 5 (page 88)

Fictional stories should be about how chewing gum was invented.

Week 2

Day 1 (page 89)

1. C
2. B
3. B
4. A

Day 2 (page 90)

1. A
2. A
3. B
4. D

Day 3 (page 91)

1. B
2. C
3. The school is celebrating by having a baking contest.
4. Answers should predict what will happen next in the story.

Day 4 (page 93)

1. A
2. C
3. A
4. C
5. *Example*
   Character: Sukun
   Setting: school at lunchtime, Sukun's home
   Problem: Sukun's friends did not want to try his Cambodian food.
   Solution: Sukun made a special recipe that was similar to cake.

Day 5 (page 94)

Book reviews should include details about the story and students' opinions of it.

Week 3

Day 1 (page 96)

1. B
2. A
3. A
4. D
5. Answers should include three clues from the text that the commercial is fake, such as the fact that no customers have reported that it works.

Day 2 (page 97)

Example Comparisons

Ruth Wakefield: baked cookies

Sukun: baked Cambodian dessert

Both: made new recipes

Day 3 (page 98)

Examples

The Invention of Gum: to describe the sequence of events that led to the invention of chewing gum

New Flavors for Old Friends: to describe the steps the character took to create his new dessert

Script for Carnadent TV Commercial: to entertain readers with a silly and humorous commercial

Day 4 (page 99)

Answers should describe in detail students' favorite foods or meals.

Answer Key *(cont.)*

Day 5 (page 100)

Written scripts for commercials should describe fictional food items or products.

Unit 6

Week 1

Day 1 (page 101)

1. C
2. B
3. C
4. C

Day 2 (page 102)

1. C
2. C
3. A
4. A

Day 3 (page 103)

1. D
2. A
3. The science of astronomy teaches us about the universe.
4. Answers should describe photos students would add to the text to help readers learn more, such as an image of a black hole.

Day 4 (page 105)

1. B
2. B
3. C
4. C

Example

Paragraph 1	stars in the night sky
Paragraph 2	constellations
Paragraph 3	constellation myths
Paragraph 4	the star Polaris
Paragraph 5	light pollution

Day 5 (page 106)

Answers should describe different connections students can make with the text.

Week 2

Day 1 (page 107)

1. B
2. C
3. A
4. C

Day 2 (page 108)

1. C
2. B
3. C
4. A

Day 3 (page 109)

1. C
2. B
3. Answers should include words from the text that show the queen is upset, such as *stormed*, *slammed her scepter*, and *screeched*.
4. Responses should describe examples of what students do that shows how they feel.

Day 4 (page 111)

1. C
2. A
3. C
4. C
5. *Example Summaries*

   Beginning—The Queen steals Loris's diamond spoon, but it doesn't work so she throws it in the sky.

   Middle—The Queen's steals Loris's second diamond spoon, but it doesn't work so she throws it in the sky.

   End—The Queen realizes the diamond spoons had nothing to do with the taste of the soup.

Day 5 (page 112)

Written responses should detail students' own versions of how the story ends.

Week 3

Day 1 (page 114)

1. B
2. B
3. D
4. B
5. Responses should state which show at the planetarium students would like to see and why.

Day 2 (page 115)

Examples

Astronomy: universe, astronomers, space, planets, stars, sun, black holes

"Astroview Planetarium": stars, tonight's sky, space robots, technology, another world, aliens

Each sentence should include a word or phrase about space from the text.

Day 3 (page 116)

Examples Comparisons

The Night Sky—purpose is to explain a constellation

A Skyful of Diamonds—purpose is to tell a fictional story about a constellation

Both—are about the Big and Little Dipper

Day 4 (page 117)

Stories should be about how a certain constellation came to be.

Day 5 (page 118)

Posters for zoos should tell about events and prices.

Unit 7

Week 1

Day 1 (page 119)

1. B
2. A
3. C
4. A

Day 2 (page 120)

1. C
2. D
3. B
4. C

Day 3 (page 121)

1. C
2. D
3. Monarch butterflies get their names from kings or queens.
4. Answers should share why students think the author wrote this text.

Answer Key *(cont.)*

Day 4 (page 123)

1. A
2. C
3. B
4. C
5. Answers should include one detail about different topics covered in the text.

Day 5 (page 124)

Responses should describe different ways humans can help monarch butterflies.

Week 2

Day 1 (page 125)

1. C
2. B
3. C
4. A

Day 2 (page 126)

1. B
2. C
3. A
4. C

Day 3 (page 127)

1. D
2. A
3. This story is a fantasy because it is not realistic for someone to grow butterfly wings.
4. Responses should include predictions students have about what happens next.

Day 4 (page 129)

1. D
2. B
3. A
4. B
5. *Example Summaries*

   Beginning—The main character is nervous about a presentation, but he gets called on first.

   Middle—The main character quickly transforms and grows butterfly wings.

   End—The main character gives his presentation, and his wings disappear.

Day 5 (page 130)

Answers should explain how the story would be different if the character became a different kind of insect.

Week 3

Day 1 (page 132)

1. B
2. A
3. A
4. C
5. Answers should share what other information students would like to see in the diagrams.

Day 2 (page 133)

Pictures should show what students visualize from reading the texts.

Day 3 (page 134)

Answers should compare and contrast the Cairns birdwing butterfly with the zebra longwing butterfly.

Day 4 (page 135)

Answers should imagine they are butterflies and describe typical days in the life of butterflies.

Day 5 (page 136)

Diagrams should include labeled drawings of insects students find interesting.

Unit 8

Week 1

Day 1 (page 137)

1. B
2. D
3. D
4. B

Day 2 (page 138)

1. D
2. B
3. B
4. A

Day 3 (page 139)

1. B
2. B
3. People hope nature preserves will help species that are dying out.
4. Answers should explain why students would or would not visit a wildlife preserve.

Day 4 (page 141)

1. C
2. D
3. B
4. C
5. Answers should include four details that explain why Iceland is a fascinating and unique country.

Day 5 (page 142)

Answers should compare Iceland to another place of students' choosing.

Week 2

Day 1 (page 143)

1. A
2. B
3. A
4. A

Day 2 (page 144)

1. B
2. D
3. B
4. A

Day 3 (page 145)

1. D
2. A
3. Mouse and Rat got to Iceland by traveling in the coat of Human Being.
4. Answers should predict what will happen next in the story.

Day 4 (page 147)

1. D
2. C
3. B
4. A
5. Answers should compare Arctic Fox and Mink. Answers may include character traits, physical appearances, and actions.

Answer Key *(cont.)*

Day 5 (page 148)

Dialogue should include a potential conversation between Arctic Fox and Mink.

Week 3

Day 1 (page 150)

1. B
2. D
3. A
4. C
5. Answers should include one or two examples of how Fannar and Brichelle are similar.

Day 2 (page 151)

Pictures should show what students visualize while reading the texts.

Day 3 (page 152)

Dialogues should show what might occur between the author of "Iceland" and Fannar.

Day 4 (page 153)

Stories should take place in Iceland, have a beginning, middle, and end, and include pictures.

Day 5 (page 154)

Email responses should be addressed to Fannar.

Unit 9

Week 1

Day 1 (page 155)

1. B
2. C
3. D
4. A

Day 2 (page 156)

1. C
2. B
3. D
4. B

Day 3 (page 157)

1. C
2. B
3. explore
4. Answers should describe images students would add to the text.

Day 4 (page 159)

1. A
2. B
3. B
4. C
5. Answers should include four events that happened on Lewis and Clark's expedition.

Day 5 (page 160)

Answers should describe what it would have been like to travel with Lewis and Clark on their expedition.

Week 2

Day 1 (page 161)

1. A
2. D
3. B
4. C

Day 2 (page 162)

1. A
2. B
3. C
4. B

Day 3 (page 163)

1. B
2. A
3. This means a place where the river splits into two different directions.
4. Answers should explain why Sacagawea should or should not go to the Shoshone camp.

Day 4 (page 165)

1. D
2. B
3. A
4. A
5. Answers should describe the narrator's feelings, character traits, relationships, and wants or needs.

Day 5 (page 166)

Journal entries should be written from the point of view of Sacagawea and describe how she is feeling and what is happening on the journey.

Week 3

Day 1 (page 168)

1. A
2. C
3. A
4. B
5. Answers should predict what students think will happen in the next scene of the play.

Day 2 (page 169)

Answers should include written dialogues between the authors of "Sacagawea's Contribution" and "November 4th, 1804."

Day 3 (page 170)

Example Comparisons

Lewis and Clark: nonfiction

Lewis and Clark Script: fiction or historical fiction, drama

Both: Lewis and Clark are the main subjects.

Day 4 (page 171)

Letters to Lewis, Clark, or Sacagawea should ask questions and detail thoughts about their lives.

Day 5 (page 172)

Scripts should try to include humor and be about students and their friends on adventures.

Unit 10

Week 1

Day 1 (page 173)

1. A
2. A
3. D
4. B

Day 2 (page 174)

1. D
2. C
3. B
4. A

Answer Key *(cont.)*

Day 3 (page 175)

1. B
2. D
3. Some animals use bioluminescence to attract prey.
4. Answers should explain why students would or would not want to be able to light up at night.

Day 4 (page 177)

1. A
2. D
3. A
4. C
5. Answers should include descriptions for each of the following deep sea creatures: vampire squid, barreleye fish, anglerfish, giant oarfish. Descriptions will vary.

Day 5 (page 178)

Answers should include descriptions and drawings of a newly discovered deep sea creature.

Week 2

Day 1 (page 179)

1. A
2. D
3. A
4. C

Day 2 (page 180)

1. B
2. A
3. C
4. C

Day 3 (page 181)

1. A
2. D
3. Cartilage is much softer than bone and it will bend under pressure instead of break.
4. Predictions should detail what will happen next in the story.

Day 4 (page 183)

1. C
2. A
3. D
4. C
5. *Example Descriptions*

   Beginning—he is excited, his skin is rough

   Middle—he grows gills and fins, his lungs are smaller, eyes are bigger, no bones

   End—he feels a little lonely, fingers are webbed, fully half-man, half-fish

Day 5 (page 184)

Answers should include the next entry of the Chimaera Log from the point of view of the narrator on day 2055.

Week 3

Day 1 (page 186)

1. B
2. C
3. A
4. D
5. Answers should include students' favorite lines from the poem and explain why they like them.

Day 2 (page 187)

Example

Text	Words or Phrases about Deep Sea Creatures
Deep Sea Creatures	cold, hard life; dazzling lights; colored bodies; grow huge
Chimaera Log: Day 1,193	senses electric fields; eyes are made to catch the faintest flash of light
Anglerfish Love Sonnet	swaying lantern; glow amidst the gloom; eyes of pearl; spikey

Day 3 (page 188)

Example Comparisons

Deep Sea Creatures: nonfiction

Anglerfish Love Sonnet: poetry

Both: about deep sea creatures

Day 4 (page 189)

Written responses should support opinions about which deep sea creature is the best.

Day 5 (page 190)

Poems should be about deep sea creatures.

Unit 11

Week 1

Day 1 (page 191)

1. A
2. C
3. C
4. A

Day 2 (page 192)

1. D
2. C
3. B
4. A

Day 3 (page 193)

1. A
2. B
3. The main idea is that you can change how you think about your problems.
4. Answers should include suggestions of solutions that could be added to the list in the text.

Day 4 (page 195)

1. C
2. D
3. C
4. A
5. Answers should include three tips the author gives for how to calm down.

Day 5 (page 196)

Answers should explain how students can use what they've learned from the text in their own lives.

Week 2

Day 1 (page 197)

1. C
2. A
3. A
4. C

Answer Key (cont.)

Day 2 (page 198)

1. B
2. D
3. A
4. B

Day 3 (page 199)

1. C
2. D
3. Niko can tell that Adaly is angry from the way she looks.

Day 4 (page 201)

1. B
2. A
3. D
4. B
5. Story maps should include details from the story.

   Example

   Characters—Adaly, Lauren, Niko

   Setting—the school playground at recess

   Conflict—Adaly gets angry that she is out, and she pushes Lauren.

   Resolution—Lauren gives Adaly space, and they talk and make up when she is calm.

Day 5 (page 202)

Answers should describe how the story might have been different if Lauren and the others did not leave Adaly alone.

Week 3

Day 1 (page 204)

1. A
2. D
3. D
4. B
5. A brother and sister fight over the last piece of chicken, and it ends up on the floor. They blame each other and then realize they were both at fault.

Day 2 (page 205)

Example

Text	Signs of Anger
Foul Play	face was clenched; body was tense; yelled; pushed
All about Anger	furrow your eyebrows; clench your teeth; muscles feel tight; can't relax; skin feels warm

Day 3 (page 206)

Example

Root of the Problem	The Last Piece of Chicken
a playground	a kitchen
friends argue about four-square	siblings fight over the last piece of chicken
friends talk and apologize	cat gets the chicken; both realize they were to blame

Day 4 (page 207)

Letters should be written to one of the characters in the story and give them advice on how to deal with anger.

Day 5 (page 208)

Comics should include pictures and/or captions detailing an original story.

Unit 12

Week 1

Day 1 (page 209)

1. D
2. A
3. A
4. C

Day 2 (page 210)

1. B
2. D
3. C
4. B

Day 3 (page 211)

1. C
2. A
3. Pilots pay attention to altitude for safety reasons.
4. Answers should describe what it would be like to fly a plane.

Day 4 (page 213)

1. C
2. C
3. B
4. D
5. Answers should include three events in Amelia Earhart's life with dates and in the order they occurred.

Day 5 (page 214)

Answers should support the opinion that Amelia Earhart was brave and courageous with details and evidence from the text.

Week 2

Day 1 (page 215)

1. C
2. A
3. C
4. A

Day 2 (page 216)

1. C
2. A
3. A
4. D

Day 3 (page 217)

1. A
2. B
3. The captain had to swerve to avoid space junk. Oosa got nauseous.
4. Answers should include predictions about what students think will happen next.

Answer Key *(cont.)*

Day 4 (page 219)

1. B
2. B
3. D
4. C
5. *Example*

Event 1	The ship nosedives toward planet Plyzon.
Event 2	They landed safely.
Event 3	They met the Space Customs agent.
Event 4	They unloaded the QualiCool Air Dye and gave it to the agent.

Day 5 (page 220)

Answers should explain why students would or would not like to be a character in this story. Reasons should be supported with evidence from the text.

Week 3

Day 1 (page 222)

1. B
2. D
3. B
4. A
5. Answers should explain whether students would or would not like to try barnstorming.

Day 2 (page 223)

Dialogues should show a discussion that might occur between Amelia Earhart and the aerobatic character in the newspaper article, *Terry Folsom*.

Day 3 (page 224)

Example Comparisons

Amelia Earhart—real person, flew airplanes

Oosa—fictional character, pilot in a spaceship

Both—flew in bad conditions, pilots

Day 4 (page 225)

Answers should explain if students would rather be real pilots of airplanes, pilots of spaceships, or aerobatic pilots. Opinions should be supported with reasons from the texts.

Day 5 (page 226)

Newspaper articles should be about Amelia Earhart's last flight.

Digital Resources

Accessing the Digital Resources

The digital resources can be downloaded by following these steps:

1. Go to **www.tcmpub.com/digital**
2. Use the 13-digit ISBN number to redeem the digital resources.
3. Respond to the question using the book.
4. Follow the prompts on the Content Cloud website to sign in or create a new account.
5. The content redeemed will appear on your My Content screen. Click on the product to look through the digital resources. All file resources are available for download. Select files can be previewed, opened, and shared.

For questions and assistance with your ISBN redemption, please contact Shell Education.

email: customerservice@tcmpub.com

phone: 800-858-7339

Contents of the Digital Resources

- Standards Correlations
- Writing Rubric
- Fluency Rubric
- Class and Individual Analysis Sheets

